UNCOVER YOUR SECRET SELF . . .

► If you had 24 hours to live, how would you spend the time?

► Is there anything you value so strongly that you would leave this country if it were taken away?

► What percentage of:

1. The defects in your home would you reveal to a prospective buyer?
2. The time do you drive over the speed limit?
3. Your time is spent doing things you really don't want to do every day?

► How would your life be different if you had a fairy godmother who could transform your appearance in whatever way you desired?

THESE QUESTIONS AND THE STIMULATING
STRATEGIES IN THIS OUTSTANDING WORKBOOK CAN
PROVIDE YOU WITH A
PRICELESS GIFT—
AN UNDERSTANDING OF YOUR TRUE SELF.

Values Clarification
A PRACTICAL, ACTION-DIRECTED WORKBOOK

VALUES
CLARIFICATION

Dr. Sidney B. Simon,

Dr. Leland W. Howe,

AND

Dr. Howard Kirschenbaum

WARNER BOOKS

A Time Warner Company

This Warner Books edition is published by arrangement with the authors.

Warner Books, Inc., 1271 Avenue of the Americas, New York, NY 10020

 A Time Warner Company

Printed in the United States of America

First Printing: September 1995

10 9 8 7 6 5 4 3 2 1

Library of Congress Cataloging-in-Publication Data

Simon, Sidney B.
    Values clarification / Sidney B. Simon, Leland W. Howe, and Howard Kirschenbaum.
      p.   cm.
    Originally published: New York : Hart Pub. Co., 1972.
    Includes index.
    ISBN 0-446-67095-2 (pbk.)
    1. Youth—Conduct of life.   2. Values clarification.   I. Howe, Leland W.   II. Kirschenbaum, Howard.   III. Title.
BJ1661.S55   1995
170'.7—dc20   95-3484
                                               CIP

Book design by Stan Drate/Folio Graphics Co. Inc.
Cover design by Wendy Bass

*This book is dedicated to Louis E. Raths.
Without his inspiring and pioneering work in
values clarification, this book could never
have been written.*

Contents

THE
VALUES-CLARIFICATION
APPROACH

Every day, every one of us meets life situations that call for thought, decision making, and action. Some of these situations are familiar, some novel; some are casual, some are of extreme importance. Everything we do, every decision we make and course of action we take, is based on our consciously or unconsciously held beliefs, attitudes, and values.

Which car shall I buy—the stripped-down model for basic transportation or the snazzy version with all the extras?

▼

Should Bill and I live together before marriage? Shouldn't we know if we're really compatible?

▼

Just how much am I willing to modify my diet to reduce fat and cholesterol? How many extra weeks of living justify my giving up ice cream and chocolate cake?

▼

What can I do to bring about political change these days?

▼

How can I find greater spirituality? Does religion have meaning in my life, or is it simply a series of outmoded traditions and customs?

▼

How important to me is my partner's physical appear-

ance? How important is my own? Can I justify spending $200 on that item of clothing?

▼

What can I do so that I don't spend my life like so many others who regret the jobs they go to every morning?

▼

Why is it that at the end of every weekend I feel anxious and guilty about all I didn't do?

▼

Shall I take early retirement?

▼

Should I ask more of my children? Am I spoiling them?

▼

What role shall I take in caring for my aging parent?

▼

This is the only life I'm going to get. How can I make it more fun?

This is a confusing world to live in. At every turn we are forced to make choices about how to live our lives. Ideally, our choices will be made on the basis of the values we hold—the principles and priorities that are important to us. But frequently we are not clear about our own values, or we are not clear about how to translate them into daily living.

Some typical areas where we may experience confusion and conflict in values are:

politics	family
religion	friends
work	money

leisure time	aging, death
school	health
love and sex	multicultural issues
material possessions	culture (art, music, and so
personal tastes (clothes,	on)
hairstyle, and so on)	

All of us, young and old, often become confused about our values. Yet today we are confronted by many more choices than in previous generations. We are surrounded by a bewildering array of alternatives. Modern society has made us less provincial and more sophisticated, but the complexity of these times has made the act of choosing infinitely more difficult.

Traditionally, our values have been formed and influenced in a variety of ways. These include:

1. Inculcation

There are numerous ways that our parents, teachers, religious institutions, workplaces, and societies attempt to instill their values and to form and influence ours. By explanation, moralizing, rules, rewards, punishments, slogans, symbols, and many other methods, from birth to death, the world around us tries to pass on and perpetuate its values.

All this is appropriate and inevitable. Civilization has learned a great deal over the millennia about how to create a social order in which people can live peaceably together, secure in their persons and property, respectful of one another's liberty, working cooperatively for the common good. Although people often do not live up to those ideals, nevertheless, we hope that they will, and we know that we should, and therefore we want to pass these values on to our children and to one another. So we do our best, as Proverbs suggests, "to train up the children in the way they should go," to pass on our most cherished values and beliefs to those whose lives we touch.

As important and inevitable as is the effort to inculcate the best values and the cultural wisdom we have developed, the approach of instilling values in others has certain limitations. One of these limitations is that there is so much diversity in the world around us. The direct inculcation of values works best when there is complete consistency about what constitutes "desirable" values. But consider the situation today. Parents offer one set of shoulds and should nots. The church often suggests another. The peer group offers a third view of values. Hollywood and the popular magazines, a fourth. The seventh-grade teacher, a fifth. The college professor, a sixth. The president of the United States, a seventh. The next president, an eighth. The spokespersons for the counterculture, a ninth, and on and on.

Bombarded by all these influences, we are ultimately left to make our own choices about whose advice or values to follow. Young people who have received effective inculcation of values will have some standards of value and right and wrong to apply in difficult choice situations, but inculcation cannot anticipate all choice situations or make some of life's most difficult choices much easier when the moment of truth arrives. And people who received little inculcation when they were young (e.g., their parents and other adults were absent, did not seem to care, or were ineffective) have an even tougher time of it. They have not learned a process for selecting the best and rejecting the worst elements contained in the various value systems that others have been urging them to follow. Thus, too often, the important choices in life are made on the basis of peer pressure, unthinking submission to authority, or the power of the mass media.

Another limitation with the direct inculcation of values is that it often results in a dichotomy between theory and practice; lip service is paid to the values of the authority or the culture, while behavior contradicts these values. Thus we have religious people who love their neighbors on the Sabbath and spend the rest of the week competing with them or downgrading them. And we have patriots who would deny freedom of speech to any dissenters whose concept of patriotism is different from theirs. And we have good, obedient students who sit quietly in class and wouldn't dare speak without raising their hands, but who freely interrupt their friends and parents in the middle of a sentence. Inculcation frequently influences only people's words and little else in their lives.

2. Modeling

The second major approach to transmitting values is modeling. The rationale here is: "I will present myself as an attractive model who lives by a certain set of values. The people with whom I come in contact will be duly impressed by me and by my values, and will want to adopt and emulate my attitudes and behavior."

Demonstrating something is almost always a more effective teaching method than simply talking about it. Modeling is so potent a means of value education because it presents a vivid example of values in action. Of course modeling operates whether we consciously work at being a model or not. We *do* notice how other people act and how they seem to negotiate life's many values choices. We also notice whether their behavior matches their stated beliefs. As positive models or negative ones, we each serve continually as models for one another. Young people in particular are hungry for role models and will find them among adults or their peers, for better or worse.

Modeling, like inculcation, is an important and inevitable form of values transmission, but like inculcation, it also has its limitations. The main problem is that people are exposed to so many different models to emulate. Parents, teachers, politicians, movie and rock stars, friends, religious figures, literary characters, and others all present different models. How is a person to sort out all the pros and cons and achieve his or her own values? How can one tell a superficially attractive model from the model with true wisdom, morality, and happiness?

So young people and adults can benefit from good inculcation and good models. We all deserve to be exposed to responsible adults who care about our welfare, teach us the best wisdom and morality they and society have accumulated over the centuries, and model a zest and joy of living. Yet when it comes time to choose an occupation, a spouse, or a candidate, how does a person choose a course of action from among the many models and many moralizing lectures with which he or she has been bombarded? Where do we learn whether to stick to the old moral and value standards or try new ones? How do we develop our own sense of identity? How do we learn to relate to people whose values differ from our own? What do we do when two important values are in conflict, and the more we choose one value the less we achieve of the other?

3. Values Clarification

The values-clarification approach tries to help people answer some of these questions and build their own value system. It is not a new approach. There have always been parents, teachers, and other educators dating at least back to Socrates who have sought ways to help people think through values issues for themselves. They have done this in many ways—by asking good questions, being a good listener, encouraging self-knowledge, and demonstrating trust in the seeker's ability to find the answer.

All these attitudes and techniques are part of the values-clarification process. However, the values-clarification approach utilized in this book is more systematic than more general techniques for encouraging introspection and personal decision making. It is based on the approach formulated by Louis Raths*, who in turn built upon the thinking of John Dewey. Unlike other theoretical approaches to values, Raths' special contribution was to focus on the *process of valuing*. His focus was on how people come to hold certain beliefs and establish certain behavior patterns.

Valuing, according to Raths, is composed of seven subprocesses:

PRIZING one's beliefs and behaviors
    1. prizing and cherishing
    2. publicly affirming, when appropriate
CHOOSING one's beliefs and behaviors
    3. choosing from alternatives
    4. choosing after consideration of consequences
    5. choosing freely

---

*Raths, Louis E., Sidney B. Simon, and Merrill Harmin, *Values and Teaching* (Columbus, OH: Charles Merrill Publishing Co., 1966).

ACTING on one's beliefs
   6. acting
   7. acting with a pattern, consistency, and repetition

In this framework, *a value* has three components—emotional, cognitive, and behavioral. Our values are based on our feelings. We don't just hold our stronger values; we care deeply and passionately about them. They are so important to us that we don't keep them hidden from the world, but in appropriate circumstances we are willing, even eager, to speak about them to others. At the same time, our values are derived by a careful process of thought, in which we evaluate the pros and cons and consequences of various choices and positions, and we strive to make choices that are our own and not the result of undue peer or authority pressure. And finally, we act upon our values. We don't just say some things are important to us, but those beliefs or preferences are clearly and consistently discernible in how we live our lives.

Values, in this sense, are distinguishable from feelings, attitudes, goals, opinions, beliefs, habits, and other "value indicators." Values are those aspects of our lives that are so important and pervasive that they include feelings, thoughts, *and* behavior. By utilizing the seven processes of valuing, we are encouraged to elevate value indicators to values, that is, to begin to act on life goals that we have hitherto only wished for, to consider alternatives to behavior patterns that are perhaps no longer satisfying, to reexamine what we really prize and cherish and to act accordingly, in short, to achieve a fuller integration of our feelings, beliefs, and behavior. Thus the values-clarification approach helps people utilize the above seven processes of values in their own lives, to apply these valuing processes to already formed beliefs and behavior patterns and to those still emerging.

Because values clarification is all about developing and acting upon one's personal values, the question often arises: Is values clarification, then, a purely selfish and amoral approach to making life's decisions? Is it only about making choices to make ourselves happy and to hell with everyone else? No, for two reasons.

First, values clarification is only one part of a more comprehensive process of values formation. We don't just make decisions on our own. We are also influenced by the inculcation and modeling we have been exposed to. People are entitled to moral and caring inculcation and to wise and effective models. We are not suggesting that parents, teachers, employers, political leaders, and others do away with inculcation and modeling, but only that these traditional methods be augmented by a more conscious and deliberate approach for helping people make their own best decisions.

Second, attention to the needs and rights of others should always be a part of the values-clarification process. An essential part of examining the consequences of any choice is to ask: What effect will this choice have on others around me? If there are moral issues involved, what is right or wrong? What is the ethical thing to do? If everyone followed my example, what kind of world would this become? If a person never had any inculcation about right and wrong and caring for others, he or she would be at a loss to answer such questions. This is why good inculcation and modeling are so important. Concepts of justice, ethics, and morality do not necessarily occur spontaneously; they must be instilled as well as discovered. So consideration of moral and ethical issues should be a part of the values-clarification process.

We believe that considerable empirical research and even greater practical experience in using the values-clarification approach over the past thirty years indicates that those who have utilized this approach in their lives have become less apathetic, less flighty, less conforming as well as less overdissenting. They are more zestful and energetic, more critical in their thinking, and are more likely to follow through on decisions. In the case of underachievers, values clarification has led to better success in school and on the job. And, as long as it is understood that the values-clarification process includes consideration of appropriate moral questions, values clarification leads not only to more personally satisfying choices in life but also to more socially constructive behavior.

▶ HOW TO USE THIS BOOK

There are several ways to use the values-clarification activities in this book:

1. As an individual. You, the reader, by yourself, can read the book, think about the many values questions and issues it raises, do the activities, and if you like, record your responses in your values journal (Strategy Number 17, page 130). It can be a purely personal experience, as you think about these issues, come to understand your feelings and beliefs more deeply, make new decisions or reaffirm old ones in your life, and begin to take action based on your values deliberations.

2. As a couple or with a friend. You can do these activities with a spouse or close friend. It's enjoyable to share your responses to the seventy-six activities and two thousand or so questions in this book. By exchanging your thoughts, feelings, and beliefs with one another, you will learn much more about yourself, each other, and the many values issues these activities raise.

3. As a family. These are wonderful activities to do with your parents and children. Many of them can easily be done around the family dinner table, on a long car ride, or on special family occasions. It is a terrific way to build family values, to share values important to family members, to have fun together, and to build a sense of family cohesiveness that derives from sharing meaningful time and conversation.

For example, one of the author's families did the Twenty Things You Love to Do activity (Strategy Number 1, page 19) on Thanksgiving Day one year. Children, parents, aunts, uncles, and grandparents were amazed and delighted to learn things about one another that they had never known before. All the generations participated and learned together. They reported it was a much more meaningful family holiday than others, when everyone rushed from the table to clean up or watch the football game.

4. As a group. Groups, clubs, work teams, and larger organizations have all derived great benefits from going through the values-clarification process together. Typically, the strategies, topics, and questions that are selected or created are relevant to the life of the group. However, many of the strategies and questions on values issues not directly related to work have also often been used to help groups and teams get to know one another as people, which builds a sense of trust and inclusion that enables the group to work more effectively together.

In family and group settings, almost all of these strategies can be applied to any age level, as long as the items are selected or adapted to the specific age level. To illustrate this point, we have provided different examples for the child, adolescent, and adult age levels for the Voting, Ranking, and Interviewing strategies (pages 25, 42, and 107–125) and the Alligator River problem (page 230).

The strategies are numbered consecutively in this book. However, the order of the strategies is more or less arbitrary. There is no hard and fast sequence that is recommended. A great deal depends on the interests of the reader or the needs and experiences of the particular group.

Each strategy is described in a standard format. First comes the purpose, which always relates to one or more of the seven processes of valuing. Then the procedures are described in detail. In many cases, additional suggestions are provided for implementing that activity in a family or group setting.

When using the activities and strategies for values clarification in group or family situations, encourage an atmosphere of openness, honesty, acceptance, and respect. If group or family members feel that something they say about their own beliefs and behavior is going to be ridiculed or held against them, they will not want to share their thoughts and feelings about values issues. One way to create this feeling of safety and respect is to always allow any family or group member to "pass," that is, to not respond to a particular question or activity. Once people know that their privacy will be respected, they are much more willing to participate honestly and openly. Another way to encourage openness and participation in family and group settings is to discourage anyone from monopolizing the discussion or speaking at too great length. If that becomes a problem, give each member a set maximum amount of time to respond (e.g., one minute each, three minutes each, and so on); this will usually facilitate greater participation and enthusiasm from all the group members.

Finally, there is nothing sacred about the particular questions and examples used throughout this book. Pick and choose the strategies, questions, and variations you like. If there are some that don't pertain to you or your group, don't use them. Even the structure of the activities, which is done for the sake of clarity and easy reference, can be changed. There is no one right way to use these strategies. Change them. Adapt them. Think of your own examples. Spend one minute in discussion or spend an hour, depending on how interested you are in the subject.

Most of all, have fun! Clarifying one's values is an exciting, lifelong process. After using these strategies with hundreds of thousands of people, we know that the activities in this book can play an enjoyable and meaningful role in helping you realize and actualize your values throughout your life.

PART
TWO

THE
VALUES-CLARIFICATION
STRATEGIES

Twenty Things You Love to Do

▶ PURPOSE

An important question to ask in the search for values is, "Am I really getting what I want out of life?" When we simply settle for whatever comes our way, rather than pursuing our own goals, we probably are not living a life based upon our own freely chosen values. We usually end up by feeling that our life is not very meaningful or satisfying. However, before we can go about building the good life, we must know what it is we value and want. This activity helps you examine your most prized and cherished activities.

▶ PROCEDURE

On a sheet of paper write the numbers from 1 to 20 down the middle of the sheet. Now make a list of *twenty things in life that you love to do*. They can be big things in life or little things. You might think in terms of the seasons of the year for things you love to do.

It is perfectly all right if you have more than twenty items or fewer than twenty items on your list.

When your list is finished, use the left-hand side of your paper to code your list in the following manner:

1. Place a dollar sign ($) beside any item that costs money to do.
2. Place a letter *A* beside those items that you prefer to do *alone*, a letter *P* next to those activities you prefer to do with other *people*, and the letters *A-P* next to activities you enjoy doing equally alone or with other people.
3. Place the letters *PL* beside those items that require *planning*.
4. Place the coding *N5* next to those items that would *not* have been listed *five* years ago.
5. Place the numbers *1* through *5* beside the five most *important* items. The best loved activity should be numbered 1, the second best, 2, and so on.
6. Indicate next to each activity *when* (day, date) you last engaged in it.

This strategy can be repeated many times throughout the years. It is a good idea to save your lists and compare them over a period of time.

Any more than five or six codings at one sitting generally overloads the circuits.

▶ **ADDITIONAL SUGGESTIONS**

You might want to add additional elements to the coding system suggested above. Here are some more suggestions that you may use or adapt:

1. Use the letter *R* for those things on your list that have an element of RISK to them. It can be physical, emotional, or intellectual risk.
2. Put an *I* next to any item that involves INTIMACY.
3. Mark with an *S* any item that can only be done in one particular SEASON of the year.
4. Put the letters *IQ* next to any item you think you would enjoy more if you were smarter.
5. Place the letter *U* next to any item you have listed that you think other people would tend to judge as UNCONVENTIONAL.
6. Put the letter *C* next to items that you think other people might judge as very CONVENTIONAL.
7. Use the code letters *MT* for items you think you will want to devote increasingly MORE TIME to in the years to come.
8. Put the letters *CH* next to the things you have listed you hope your own CHILDREN would have on their own lists someday.
9. Which items on your list do you feel nobody would conceivably REJECT you for loving? Code them with the letters *RE*.
10. Place the letter *O* next to any items you would rather do OUTSIDE. Place the letters *IN* next to any items you would rather do INSIDE.
11. Put an *MI* by any of your items that you would not be able to do if you moved a thousand MILES south from where you now live.
12. Choose three items you want to become really BETTER at doing. Put the letter *B* next to these items.
13. Which of the items that you put on your list would

you want to see on a list made by the person you love the very most? Mark these items with an *L*.

14. Next to each item write the name of a person you want most to talk to about that specific item.

15. Write the letter *F* next to those items that you think will not appear on your list five years from now.

Values Grid

▸ PURPOSE

The values grid usually drives home the point that few of our beliefs or actions fit all seven of the valuing processes. This activity indicates what steps we must take in order to develop stronger and clearer values.

▸ PROCEDURE

Construct a values grid as shown below:

ISSUE	1	2	3	4	5	6	7
1							
2							
3							
4							
5							
ETC.							

Then name some general topical issues, such as energy, water pollution, population control, abortion, race relations, a specific election, a school issue, and so on. List these issues on the lines on the left-hand side of your paper. Next to each of these general issues write privately a few key words that summarize your position or stand on each issue.

The seven numbers heading the columns on the right-hand side of the paper represent the following seven questions:

1. Are you *proud* of (do you prize or cherish) your position?
2. Have you *publicly affirmed* your position?
3. Have you chosen your position from *alternatives*?
4. Have you chosen your position after *thoughtful consideration* of the pros and cons and consequences?
5. Have you chosen your position *freely*?
6. Have you *acted* on or done anything about your beliefs?
7. Have you acted with *repetition*, pattern, or consistency on this issue?

Then answer each of these seven questions in relation to each issue. If you have a positive response to the question on top, put a check in the appropriate box. If you cannot answer the question affirmatively, leave the box blank.

You might want to save your grid and look at it again at some future date. You will be able to see not only whether the content of your beliefs has undergone any change, but, just as important, whether there have been any changes in the quality and degree of your convictions.

Values Voting

▸ PURPOSE

Voting provides a simple and very rapid means by which we can consider a variety of values issues. When done in a family or group setting, it develops the realization that others often see issues quite differently than we ourselves do and legitimizes that important fact.

▸ PROCEDURE

If you are doing this activity by yourself, put a *y* for "yes" on the line to the left of each description if you think the description fits you, you agree with it, or you can answer in the affirmative. Put an *n* for "no" on the line to the left of each description if you think the description does not fit you, you disagree, or you would answer negatively. If your response is strongly positive (e.g., that's you all over) or strongly negative (e.g., you would *never* consider doing this), use a capital *Y* or *N* to indicate your response. If you can't decide, leave the item blank. Answer as many questions as you wish.

In a group or family setting, a volunteer reads aloud one by one questions that begin with the words, "How many of you . . . ?" For example, "How many of you like to go on long walks or hikes?" After each question is read, people take a position by a show of hands. Those who wish to answer in the affirmative raise their hands. Those who choose to answer negatively point their thumbs down. Those who are undecided fold their arms. And those who want to pass simply take no action at all. Discussion is tabled until the leader has completed the entire list.

Voting is an excellent way to introduce specific values issues in a group or family setting. For example, you might want to raise values issues on race relations. A voting list made of questions about people's feelings, thoughts, and actions on race-related issues (e.g., How many of you . . . have ever visited in the home of a friend of different race? Think that black people and white people are different beyond skin color?) provides an effective way to stimulate interest.

Once people get the hang of voting, they can create excellent voting lists of their own. They can make up lists of questions about their own concerns and then conduct the voting themselves.

Voting lists should not be too long. They lose their effectiveness after about ten or more items. Discussion may or may not follow.

The leader votes, too. To keep from influencing the vote, the leader holds his or her vote until a split second after most of the others have committed themselves to a position.

In some cases, the leader might want to vary the voting procedure. For example, he or she might want to add the following statement to the voting directions: "On some issues you may have *very strong* feelings—for or against. If you have a very positive response to a question, you may show this by waving your raised hand. If you have a very negative response, you may choose to show this by pointing your thumb down and moving your arm up and down for emphasis."

Sometimes the leader may ask if anyone would care to choose one of the questions and discuss his or her reaction to it.

▸ VALUES VOTING LISTS

We have provided many examples of questions for values voting lists. The following questions listed are divided into four categories. The first listing is general and may be used for most ages except the very youngest. The next list is most appropriate for older adolescents and adults, although some of the questions may be used at younger levels. The adolescents list is most suitable for pre- and early adolescents, although many of the questions are appropriate for older adolescents and adults as well. The children's list is most appropriate for young children.

Many of the questions can be reworded and used in other values strategies. For example, by placing the words "Have you ever . . ." or some other appropriate beginning in front of some of the items, the questions can be used with the Interviewing strategies (Numbers 12–14, pages 107–125).

Each of the questions below should be prefaced by the statement "How many of you . . ." or "How many here. . . ."

EXAMPLES FOR GENERAL USE WITH ALL AGES

1. ____ enjoy watching movies on TV?
2. ____ go to church or temple regularly?
3. ____ enjoy going to church or temple?
4. ____ think children should have to work for their allowance?
5. ____ have ever been in love?
6. ____ are in love right now?
7. ____ have ever felt lonely even in a crowd of people?
8. ____ have a close friend of another race?
9. ____ have had someone from another race to your house for dinner or to a play?
10. ____ would like to bring in a voting list tomorrow?
11. ____ have learned something from a person eight years or younger in the past year?
12. ____ have a favorite hobby or pastime?
13. ____ feel that religion is an important part of your life?
14. ____ think students are losing respect for teachers?
15. ____ think you are racially prejudiced?
16. ____ think familiarity breeds contempt?
17. ____ wish you were home right now doing whatever you like to do?
18. ____ think that at this point in your life you are a complete flop or failure?
19. ____ think that we should have spent all that money to go to the moon?
20. ____ would like to go into politics someday?
21. ____ have ever personally witnessed a violent act?
22. ____ have ever participated in a litter pick-up day?
23. ____ have ever had problems so bad you wished you could die so you wouldn't have to face them?

24. ___ are in favor of having American police follow the example of traditional British bobbies—no live ammunition?

25. ___ would live forever if you could?

26. ___ think more federal aid should be given to welfare programs?

27. ___ think abortion is morally wrong?

28. ___ are in favor of the death penalty?

29. ___ think that women should stay home and be primarily wives and mothers? Men . . . husbands and fathers?

30. ___ think that most young people feel free to talk with their parents?

31. ___ think most students feel free to talk with their teachers?

32. ___ find it difficult to listen to people sometimes?

33. ___ have a clear idea of your own values?

34. ___ have ever had a scary dream?

35. ___ have read a book just for fun in the last month?

36. ___ play a musical instrument?

37. ___ enjoy going on a picnic?

38. ___ have ever daydreamed in school?

39. ___ have been hurt by a friend?

40. ___ are an only child?

41. ___ have/had a favorite game as a child?

42. ___ would favor a law to limit families to two children?

43. ___ often think of death?

44. ___ would like to make some changes in your life?

45. ___ have ever gone skiing?

46. ___ think there are times when cheating is justified?

47. ___ think it is alright for older brothers and sisters to discipline younger ones?

48. ___ would like to go to the moon someday?
49. ___ think that most people cheat on something?
50. ___ sometimes have secrets you don't even tell your best friends?
51. ___ would like to have a celebrity as a friend?
52. ___ would rather be older or younger than you are now?
53. ___ like to do things with your family?
54. ___ think most adults understand young people today?
55. ___ would like to be president? A senator? A Supreme Court judge?
56. ___ have ever been to Europe? To another state in the United States?
57. ___ have a special place of your own?
58. ___ have lived in the city (country, suburbs) all your life?
59. ___ would rather live someplace else?
60. ___ know someone who has fought in a war?
61. ___ have watched a sunrise with someone this past year? A sunset?
62. ___ have slept in a tent this year?
63. ___ wear seat belts when riding in a car?
64. ___ would be willing to donate your body to science when you die?
65. ___ think school attendance ought to be optional?
66. ___ enjoy giving gifts?
67. ___ would like to grow a beard or mustache?
68. ___ give money to at least one charity?
69. ___ like yogurt?
70. ___ would rather work alone?
71. ___ have written a letter to your congressperson or the president?

72. ____ knew someone who died of AIDS?
73. ____ own a horse?
74. ____ would like to jump from a plane with a parachute?
75. ____ have had a snowball fight?
76. ____ enjoy family meals with TV in the background?
77. ____ think you will be only too happy to retire when the time comes?
78. ____ think the job of parenting should be shared by all adults?
79. ____ play sports with your family?
80. ____ get enough sleep at night?
81. ____ usually don't sleep very well at night? Have trouble going to sleep?
82. ____ enjoy taking walks?
83. ____ think there should be a law guaranteeing a minimum income?
84. ____ have difficulty sitting still for more than an hour?
85. ____ wouldn't mind having classes with no textbooks?
86. ____ enjoy playing a musical instrument?
87. ____ think teenagers should not go steady?
88. ____ think that the way you view death is related to the way you view life?
89. ____ have ever visited someone in a hospital?
90. ____ would like to take karate lessons?
91. ____ think students should pay their own way through college?
92. ____ would like to own a sailboat?
93. ____ think that the father should have as much responsibility for parenting as the mother?

94. ___ think that communication is more open in families today?

95. ___ dream of owning a sports car?

96. ___ consciously try to save energy by turning your lights out when they're not needed?

97. ___ are happy in your work?

98. ___ would like your body to be cremated when you die?

99. ___ think capital punishment should be abolished?

100. ___ would like to take early retirement at age forty? Fifty?

101. ___ think we should take more trips to other planets?

102. ___ could invite someone you couldn't stand to your home?

103. ___ are fully satisfied with what you have accomplished in life so far?

104. ___ would play the stock market with your savings?

105. ___ think we ought to legalize "pot" (marijuana)?

106. ___ approve of free choice on abortion?

107. ___ think you should have to pass a test or get a license to be a parent?

108. ___ think we ought to have compulsory school attendance until age sixteen?

109. ___ think we ought to raise the voting age to twenty-one?

110. ___ think you are a well-organized person?

111. ___ know the contents of your top dresser drawer?

112. ___ would turn in a drug pusher to the law? Even if he/she were your friend?

113. ___ would turn in someone for using drugs? Even if he/she were your friend?

114. ___ have ever wanted to seek revenge for something someone did to you?
115. ___ have ever written a letter to the editor?
116. ___ have ever written a Dear John letter? Received one?
117. ___ think homosexuality should be against the law?
118. ___ think it is all right for men to wear wigs?
119. ___ used to be hall monitors in elementary school?
120. ___ spend less than $100 total for Christmas or holiday presents?
121. ___ have more than five pairs of shoes?
122. ___ think that teachers shouldn't say "hell" or "damn" in the classroom?
123. ___ have full polio protection?
124. ___ like to read the comics first thing in the Sunday paper?
125. ___ belong to a Christmas saving club?
126. ___ make some of the gifts you give at Christmas/ holidays?
127. ___ have not been invited to a party you wanted to go to?
128. ___ feel that all of your family members feel they are a part of decision making in the home?
129. ___ didn't have any cavities the last time you went to the dentist?
130. ___ have ever signed a petition?
131. ___ have ever broken an arm or leg?
132. ___ have not yet made plans for the coming summer?
133. ___ have ever caught a mouse in a mousetrap?
134. ___ are willing to admit when you are wrong?
135. ___ spend most of your time out of doors in nice weather?

136. ____ have hurt feelings when you are criticized?

137. ____ don't like to show that you're angry?

FOR USE WITH OLDER ADOLESCENTS AND ADULTS

1. ____ feel that the feminist movement has had a mostly positive influence?

2. ____ think giving grades in school encourages meaningful learning?

3. ____ think it's best to remain a virgin until you're married?

4. ____ approve of premarital sex?

5. ____ would prefer a girl or a boy to marry someone from his or her own race?

6. ____ think sex education should be taught in the schools?

7. ____ think sex education instruction in the schools should include techniques for lovemaking? Contraception?

8. ____ think today's kids are more courageous, adventurous, wise, involved, and concerned with life than the previous generations?

9. ____ think that teachers should discuss their personal lives with students?

10. ____ have recently begun a family tradition?

11. ____ think school administrators should be selected from the teaching staff on a rotating basis?

12. ____ think merit pay is a good thing?

13. ____ would approve of a marriage between homosexuals being sanctioned by priest, minister, or rabbi?

14. ____ would approve of a young couple trying out

marriage by living together for six months before actually getting married?

15. ____ have worked together as a family on a social
issue?

16. ____ think that children ought to compete in school
to prepare them for the "real" world after gradu-
ation?

17. ____ think that most schools today are exciting
places?

18. ____ think that your school is an exciting place
for students?

19. ____ think that most students have a clear idea of
their values in life?

20. ____ think that the curriculum in most schools is
designed for teachers rather than students?

21. ____ have a part-time job?

22. ____ would like teachers to be called by their first
names?

23. ____ would like to change your profession/college/
major/occupation if you had a chance?

24. ____ like to spend time with children?

25. ____ would encourage abortion for an unwed
daughter?

26. ____ have spoken with homosexuals about their lifestyle?

27. ____ would change to a job you really didn't like if it
offered $10,000 a year more than you now
make?

28. ____ think it's fun to learn new things?

29. ____ keep a compost pile?

30. ____ meditate?

31. ____ watch your weight?

32. ____ approve of people marrying in their teens?

33. ___ think that schools do not prepare young people well enough for life?

34. ___ think that teachers should transmit their own values to students?

35. ___ would take your children to religious services even if they didn't want to go?

36. ___ think you would change your lifestyle if your income were doubled?

37. ___ would actively participate in a fair-housing movement in your community if someone got the ball started?

38. ___ would approve of contract marriages in which the marriage would come up for renewal every few years?

39. ___ would be upset if your daughter were living with a man who had no intentions of marriage? If your son were living with a woman who had no intentions of marriage?

40. ___ enjoy smoking?

41. ___ would be upset if organized religion disappeared?

42. ___ think the government should help support day-care centers for working mothers?

43. ___ think that parents should be subsidized to pick any school they want for their children?

44. ___ think grades (marking) ought to be abolished in school?

45. ___ would be in favor of a halfway house for drug addicts in your neighborhood?

46. ___ think that the role of paraprofessionals in medicine should be expanded?

47. ___ think there is nothing morally wrong with using the pill for birth control?

48. ___ watch the checker in the supermarket to see if mistakes are made?

49. ___ would not hesitate to marry someone from a different religion? From another race? Ethnic group?

50. ___ have ever participated in a demonstration? Carried a picket sign?

51. ___ ride your bike to work/school?

52. ___ would approve of another adult reprimanding your child for using abusive language?

53. ___ think it's okay to dye your hair a different color?

54. ___ expect to get a doctorate someday?

55. ___ own a credit card?

56. ___ have purchased a hardbound book that was not a text in the past year?

57. ___ have grown up on a farm?

58. ___ want to give or receive an engagement ring? Want it to be a diamond?

59. ___ subscribe to a magazine?

60. ___ collect savings stamps? Actually paste and trade them in?

61. ___ have ever taken a sex education course?

62. ___ have ever sent in money to a TV telethon?

63. ___ think that the young people of today are spoiled?

64. ___ give money to a beggar?

65. ___ pick up hitchhikers?

66. ___ have ever tended a garden?

67. ___ will never spank your children?

68. ___ frequently burn candles at home?

69. ___ would approve of a couple using artificial insemination if the husband were sterile?

70. ___ watch the Super Bowl every year?

71. ___ keep a journal or diary?
72. ___ would like to take up glider soaring?
73. ___ think we should legalize mercy killings?
74. ___ think teenagers should be allowed to choose their own clothes?
75. ___ would raise your children more strictly than you were raised?
76. ___ watch TV more than three hours per day?
77. ___ think the most qualified person usually wins in school elections?
78. ___ like to watch a religious program on TV on Sunday?
79. ___ could tell someone they have bad breath?
80. ___ think going steady is important in order to achieve social success?
81. ___ regularly attend religious services and enjoy them?

FOR USE WITH PRE- AND EARLY ADOLESCENTS

1. ___ dream about being famous?
2. ___ have ever cheated on an exam?
3. ___ jog regularly?
4. ___ have ever wished you were a child again?
5. ___ would smoke a marijuana cigarette if it were offered to you?
6. ___ would love to direct a large symphony orchestra someday?
7. ___ have ever finished a piece of furniture?
8. ___ would stay at a party where marijuana was being smoked?
9. ___ have a poster on a wall at home?
10. ___ think your teachers are not strict enough?

11. ___ would go to school if you didn't have to?
12. ___ almost never fight with your brothers and sisters?
13. ___ would like to change something about your school?
14. ___ would like to earn some money?
15. ___ would like to be a marine someday?
16. ___ answer the phone differently sometimes just for fun?
17. ___ use an alarm clock to wake up in the morning?
18. ___ would like to ride a motorcycle?
19. ___ don't like to talk in class?
20. ___ would mind if your teacher were a sloppy dresser?
21. ___ have bought something in a store and asked not to receive the paper bag?
22. ___ plan on going to college?
23. ___ have a brother or sister in college?
24. ___ have a TV set in your bedroom?
25. ___ would like to be voted best liked in the class?
26. ___ have a clothing allowance and are allowed to purchase your own clothes?
27. ___ have your own bedroom?
28. ___ would like to have the same teacher(s) next year?
29. ___ enjoy blizzards?
30. ___ subscribe to a magazine that comes addressed to you?
31. ___ have ever visited your father's place of work? Your mother's?
32. ___ got something for Christmas that was advertised on TV?
33. ___ have a best friend of the opposite sex?

34. ____ would like to be a member of the safety patrol?
35. ____ would like to call your teacher by his/her first name?
36. ____ would like to live in another country?
37. ____ would like to stay on a deserted island by yourself for a week?
38. ____ have read a children's book to a younger person in the past week?
39. ____ think that girls and boys should be in separate classrooms?
40. ____ would like to change your hairstyle?
41. ____ would ask your parents to stop smoking?
42. ____ do some kind of volunteer work?
43. ____ have ever been a scout?
44. ____ know someone who has been very sick or has died from drugs?
45. ____ know what you would like to do when you finish school?

EXAMPLES FOR USE WITH YOUNGER CHILDREN

1. ____ have a pet at home?
2. ____ have a favorite movie star?
3. ____ would like to live on a farm?
4. ____ would like to live in a different city someday?
5. ____ like chocolate ice cream?
6. ____ like asparagus?
7. ____ think school is fun?
8. ____ have a favorite TV show?
9. ____ wish you could stay up later at night?
10. ____ like to go on long car trips?
11. ____ have a best friend?

12. ___ would rather play in a baseball game than watch one?
13. ___ have ever climbed a mountain?
14. ___ daydream sometimes?
15. ___ think you will smoke cigarettes someday?
16. ___ have been to the movies in the past two weeks?
17. ___ would rather go to the movies than to school?
18. ___ like to be teased?
19. ___ sometimes tease others?
20. ___ receive an allowance?
21. ___ have to work for your allowance?
22. ___ would like to change your name?
23. ___ would like to have an important job someday?
24. ___ can swim?
25. ___ would like your parents to have a baby?
26. ___ go to Sunday School or religious class?
27. ___ would like to go to Disneyland?
28. ___ think teachers should be allowed to spank you?
29. ___ have a private place to go when you want to be alone?
30. ___ have a friend or relative in a foreign country?
31. ___ like to sing to yourself?
32. ___ watch *Sesame Street*?
33. ___ are afraid of the dark? Earthquakes? Your teacher?
34. ___ are members of a Brownie troop or Cub pack?
35. ___ like frozen custard better than regular ice cream?
36. ___ think that it is all right for girls to play with Hot Wheels?
37. ___ think that it is all right for boys to play with Barbie dolls?

Rank Order

► PURPOSE

Each day of our lives we must make choices between competing alternatives. Some of them are minor decisions: "Shall I stay home tonight and watch TV or go to a friend's house for the evening?" And some are major decisions: "Shall I buy a car or save for my children's college education?"

This strategy gives you practice in choosing from among alternatives. When done in a family or group setting it gives practice in publicly affirming and explaining or defending your choices. It demonstrates simply and clearly that many issues require more thoughtful consideration than we tend to give them.

► PROCEDURES

Select a dozen or so rank order questions from the age appropriate list. Then rank order the alternatives for each question according to your preference by placing a 1 next to your number one preference, a 2 next to your second, and so on. Be sure to rank *all* the choices from first to last.

To use in a family or group setting, the leader explains that he or she is going to ask some questions that will require a value judgment. The leader then reads a question and calls upon people in turn to give their rankings. Each person quickly gives all his or her rankings, from first to last. Of course, people may say, "I pass." After others have responded to a question, the leader may give his or her own rankings. Then a discussion may follow, with people explaining their reasons for their choices and mentioning additional choices they would prefer that were not among the options given.

▶ RANK ORDER QUESTIONS

Below are examples of rank order questions for use at various age levels.

FOR GENERAL USE

1. Which is most important in a friendship?

_____ loyalty

_____ generosity

_____ honesty

2. Which season do you like best?

_____ winter

_____ spring

_____ summer

_____ fall

3. If I gave you $500, what would you do with it?

_____ save it

_____ give it to charity

_____ buy something for myself

4. Which do you think is most harmful?

_____ cigarettes

_____ marijuana

_____ alcohol

5. How late should fourteen-year-olds be allowed to stay out on a weekend night?

_____ 10 P.M.

_____ 12 P.M.

_____ it's up to them

6. If you were a parent, how late would _you_ let your fourteen-year-old stay out?

_____ 10 P.M.

_____ 12 P.M.

_____ it's up to him/her

7. Where would you rather live?

_____ on a farm

_____ in the suburbs

_____ in a city

8. Which do you like best?

_____ winter in the mountains

_____ summer by the sea

_____ autumn in the country

9. Which would you rather be?

_____ an only child

_____ the youngest child

_____ the oldest child

10. Which pet would you rather have?

_____ a cat

_____ a dog

_____ a turtle

_____ a parakeet

11. If you were president, which would you give the highest priority?

    _____ space program

    _____ poverty program

    _____ defense program

    _____ national health care program

12. Which would you *least* like to be?

    _____ very poor

    _____ very sickly

    _____ disfigured

13. Whom would you prefer to marry? A person with

    _____ intelligence

    _____ personality

    _____ sex appeal

14. Which do you think more money should be spent on?

    _____ space station

    _____ slum clearance

    _____ cure for cancer

15. What would you be most likely to do about a person who has bad breath?

    _____ directly tell them

    _____ send them an anonymous note

    _____ nothing

16. Which would you rather have happen to you if you had bad breath?

    _____ be told directly

    _____ receive an anonymous note

    _____ not be told

17. When you worry about your mark on an exam do you think about

    _____ yourself?

    _____ your parents?

_____ pleasing the teacher?

_____ getting into college?

18. Which type of teacher do you most prefer?

_____ strict in the classroom but little homework

_____ strict in the classroom and much homework

_____ easygoing in the classroom but much homework

19. Which would you least like to do?

_____ listen to a Beethoven symphony

_____ watch a debate

_____ watch a play

20. Which would you most like to improve?

_____ your looks

_____ the way you use your time

_____ your social life

21. How do you have the most fun?

_____ alone

_____ with a large group

_____ with a few friends

22. If you had $500 to spend on decorating a room, would you spend

_____ $200 for a painting, the rest on furniture?

_____ $400 on furniture and $100 for a painting?

_____ entire sum on furniture?

23. You are married and have your own family. Your mother has died and your father is old. What would you do?

_____ invite him to live in your home

_____ place him in a home for the aged

_____ get him an apartment for himself

24. Which would you rather your sister gave you for your birthday?

　　　_____ $5 to buy yourself something

　　　_____ a $5 gift of her choice

　　　_____ something she made for you

25. If someone's parents were in constant conflict, which would be better for them to do?

　　　_____ get divorced and the father leave home

　　　_____ stay together and hide their feelings for the sake of the children

　　　_____ get divorced and the children live with their father

26. What would you do for your parents' anniversary?

　　　_____ buy them a nice present

　　　_____ make them a big party

　　　_____ take them out to dinner and a show

27. If you had two hours to spend with a friend, which would you prefer to do?

　　　_____ hang out together

　　　_____ go to a movie

　　　_____ go for a walk

　　　_____ go to a sports event

　　　_____ play a game

28. You've spent a great deal of time picking a gift for a friend. You give it to him or her personally. What would you rather have him or her do if he or she doesn't like the gift?

　　　_____ keep the gift and thank you politely

　　　_____ tell you he doesn't like it

　　　_____ return the gift to the store without telling you

29. If you supported a particular war and you found out your friend was a pacifist, would you

　　　_____ discontinue the relationship?

_____ overlook the discrepancy in views?

_____ try to change his/her viewpoint?

30. Which would you rather do?

_____ hike up a mountain with a good trail but difficult grade

_____ blaze a new trail through the woods

_____ hike on a fairly level, well-marked trail

31. Which would be the best method to alleviate the population problem?

_____ limit each family to two children and sterilize the parents afterward

_____ keep abortion legal

_____ distribute birth control information everywhere

_____ trust people's common sense to limit the size of their families

32. Imagine you are living with a family of a different religion for a few months. At meals they say a grace that is affiliated with a religion different from yours. Would you

_____ join in

_____ sit silently

_____ try to get them to change the grace to a more universal one

33. What would you think if you saw a speaker burning a dollar bill to make a point?

_____ that the man is foolish

_____ that the man has integrity

_____ why doesn't the man give that dollar to me?

34. If you suddenly inherited money and became a millionaire, would you

_____ share your wealth through charities, educational trust funds, and so on?

_____ continue in your present job and activities?

_____ really live it up?

35. If you had $20 you didn't need for something else, would you

_____ get a newspaper subscription?

_____ buy another shirt or blouse?

_____ treat a friend to dinner?

36. You are well off financially and you inherit $10,000. What would you do?

_____ put it in a savings bank

_____ invest it all in the stock market

_____ spend it all

37. Which would be your job preference?

_____ hard and dirty work at $600 per week

_____ clean and easy work at $300 per week

_____ dirty but easy work at $450 per week

38. Which do you most want money for?

_____ to buy your own food and clothing

_____ to go places on your own

_____ to feel independent

39. Where would you seek help in a strange city?

_____ a church

_____ a police station

_____ a people's community center

40. Which would you find easiest to do?

_____ campaign for contributions to a Thanksgiving food drive

_____ tutor other students

_____ be a hospital volunteer worker

41. Which would you be most willing to do to save energy?

_____ install a solar heating system

_____ turn down the thermostat to sixty-five
degrees and wear sweaters

_____ move to a warmer climate

42. Which would you be least willing to do?

_____ join a picket line

_____ take part in a sit-in

_____ sign a petition

43. In your leisure time, what would you most like to do?

_____ weave, make pottery, or do some craft

_____ play a guitar

_____ water-ski

44. What is the most serious problem in this city today?

_____ health

_____ discrimination in jobs and housing

_____ transportation

_____ hunger

_____ drugs

_____ crime

45. What is the most serious domestic issue in the United
States today?

_____ spouse and child abuse

_____ crime prevention

_____ welfare

_____ health

46. Which would you most like to be?

_____ owner of a small business

_____ employee in a large corporation

_____ employee in a small business

47. Which would you most like to see?

_____ integration of races

_____ separate nations for different races

_____ separate areas within existing communi-
ties for each race

48. Which would you least like to be?

    _____ a rifleman firing point-blank at the charging enemy

    _____ a bomber on a plane dropping bombs on an enemy village

    _____ a helicopter pilot directing a naval bombardment of enemy troops

49. Where would you most like to visit?

    _____ England

    _____ Russia

    _____ China

    _____ South Africa

    _____ Brazil

50. Which would you prefer?

    _____ a short, exciting life with a peaceful death

    _____ a long, dull life with a peaceful death

    _____ a long, exciting life with a painful death

51. Which do you like to do most?

    _____ play tennis

    _____ play football

    _____ swim

52. Which would you like to do most?

    _____ learn to skin-dive

    _____ learn to ride a mini-bike

    _____ learn to ride a horse

53. Which would you like to do most?

    _____ travel by automobile

    _____ travel by bus

    _____ travel by airplane

    _____ travel by train

54. Which would you like to do most?

    _____ learn to fly an airplane

_____ learn to drive a car

_____ learn to ride a motorcycle

55. Which would you like to do most?

_____ shoot a high-powered rifle

_____ shoot a shotgun

_____ shoot arrows

_____ not shoot at all

56. Which would you like to do most?

_____ become a jet fighter pilot

_____ become an astronaut

_____ become a surgeon

57. Which do you like most?

_____ math

_____ English

_____ social studies

58. Which do you like best?

_____ Jell-O

_____ pie

_____ ice cream

59. Which would you prefer to be?

_____ a prison guard

_____ a garbage collector

_____ an assembly-line worker

60. Which would you least like to be?

_____ a hangman

_____ a member of a firing squad

_____ the person who pulls the switch for the electric chair

61. Whom do you like least?

_____ a shoplifter

_____ a drug pusher

_____ a confidence man

62. What is the most serious problem in your school?

_____ apathy

_____ drugs

_____ discipline

63. Which would you be most willing to do?

_____ serve in the armed forces

_____ serve in the Peace Corps

_____ work in an urban ghetto

64. In which of these situations would you be most likely to take some action?

_____ a car is parked with its headlights on in broad daylight

_____ a dog has scared a kitten up a telephone pole

_____ some tough kids are trying to tie tin cans to the tail of a dog

65. How would you spend an inheritance?

_____ on travel

_____ on education

_____ on entertainment

66. Which would you least like to be?

_____ deaf

_____ an amputee

_____ blind

67. What would you most like to do with your friends during your leisure time?

_____ play a sport or game

_____ go to the movies or watch TV

_____ just talk

_____ play cards

68. Which death do you consider the greatest loss?

_____ Martin Luther King's

_____ John F. Kennedy's

_____ Malcolm X's
_____ Robert Kennedy's

FOR USE WITH OLDER ADOLESCENTS AND ADULTS

1. If you were with your family in a boat that capsized far from shore and there was only one life preserver, would you
   _____ save your wife/husband?
   _____ save one of your children?
   _____ save yourself?

2. If you were stranded on a deserted island, which would you rather have with you?
   _____ the Bible
   _____ the complete works of Shakespeare
   _____ the history of civilization

3. Which of these would be most difficult for you to accept?
   _____ the death of a parent
   _____ the death of a spouse
   _____ your own death

4. How would you break off a three-year relationship with someone you've been dating steadily?
   _____ by telephone
   _____ by mail
   _____ in person

5. Which of these jobs would you like most?
   _____ schoolteacher on an Indian reservation
   _____ director of an inner city project
   _____ coordinator of social action projects for a liberal suburban church

6. What is the worst thing you could find out about your teenager? (Does the sex make any difference?)
   _____ that he/she has been shoplifting

_____ that he/she is a high school dropout

_____ that he/she is promiscuous

7. Which would you be more concerned about as you grow older?

_____ lung cancer

_____ being overweight

_____ declining vision

8. Would you rather be a teacher in the

_____ 1950s?

_____ 1960s/'70s?

_____ 1990s?

9. As a small child, which did you like least?

_____ recess

_____ show and tell

_____ story time

10. Which would you prefer to give up if you had to?

_____ economic freedom

_____ religious freedom

_____ political freedom

11. If you needed help in your studies, whom would you probably go to?

_____ your friend

_____ your teacher

_____ your parent

12. Which of these problems do you think is the greatest threat in the nearest future?

_____ overpopulation

_____ too much leisure time

_____ water and air pollution

_____ crime

_____ AIDS

13. During a campus protest where would you be most likely to be found?

_____ in the midst of it

_____ watching it from across the street

_____ in the library minding your own business

14. Which would you rather see a cutback of federal expenditures for?

_____ social services

_____ education

_____ foreign aid

15. During what period in U.S. history do you think you would have been the most effective leader?

_____ colonization of America

_____ Civil War

_____ the Industrial Revolution

16. How would you rather spend a Saturday evening?

_____ at a good play

_____ at a good concert

_____ at a good movie

17. How would you rather spend a Friday evening?

_____ at a nightclub

_____ at home alone

_____ at a party at a friend's home

18. Which would you least like your son or daughter to do?

_____ marry out of necessity

_____ marry outside of his/her race

_____ smoke marijuana once a week

19. If the country were fighting a war you opposed and you were about to be drafted into the army, which would you do?

_____ enter the army

_____ leave the country

_____ go to jail

20. Which is the most beautiful sight to you?

_____ a sunset

_____ a person giving blood

_____ a baby taking his/her first step

21. Which do you like least?

_____ an uptight indoctrinator

_____ a cynical debunker

_____ a dull, boring fact giver

22. Which would you most like to take a course in?

_____ sex education

_____ race relations

_____ ecology

_____ drug abuse education

23. Which would you first join?

_____ a women's/men's consciousness-raising group

_____ an environmental action group

_____ a community food cooperative

24. Which of these people would you have the most trouble introducing to your friends?

_____ a racially mixed couple

_____ a person who has changed their sex

_____ the Grand Dragon of the Ku Klux Klan

25. Which best discribes the way you handle money?

_____ spend freely

_____ always look for bargains

_____ budget carefully

26. If one of your friends and your spouse were attracted to each other, which would you prefer?

_____ for them to be open about their relationship

_____ for no one to know

_____ for them to keep it a secret from you alone

27. Which would you want most in a best friend?

_____ someone who will tell you that your fiancée isn't good enough for you

———— someone who will listen to your problems

———— someone who is aware of other people's needs

28. Your friend has written a book that you think is lousy. If he asks for your opinion, what would you tell him?

———— the whole truth

———— as much as you think he can stand

———— what he wants to hear

29. *Men.* What kind of wife would bother you most?

———— one who interrupts her husband

———— one who spends too much money

———— one who keeps a messy house

30. *Women.* What kind of husband would bother you most?

———— one who interrupts his wife

———— one who spends too much money

———— one who keeps a messy house

31. *Teenagers.* Which do you think is the worst?

———— to become (or get someone) pregnant (unwed)

———— to be dependent upon hard drugs

———— to date someone from another race

———— to date someone from another religion

32. Where would you rather be on a Saturday afternoon?

———— at the beach

———— in the woods

———— in a discount store

33. How do you learn best?

———— through lectures

———— through independent study

———— through seminars

34. Which would you rather be?

———— a black American

———— a black African

———— a black European

35. Which would you give the lowest priority to today?

———— space

———— poverty

———— defense

———— ecology

———— health

36. Which of these would you want least as a neighbor?

———— a former thief

———— a former child molester

———— a former pyromaniac

FOR USE WITH PREADOLESCENTS AND CHILDREN

1. Which kind of teacher would you prefer?

———— a nasty person but a good teacher

———— a nice person but a poor teacher

———— personality and teaching ability about average

2. Which do you like least?

———— a classmate who plays practical jokes on you

———— a classmate who constantly tattles

———— a classmate who gossips about other people

3. What kind of present would you like most to get?

———— a surprise present

———— a present you already know about

———— a present you pick out

4. To whom would you tell a secret?

———— your friend

———— your teacher

———— your parent

5. What would you consider the worst experience?
   _____ telling on a best friend
   _____ changing schools
   _____ getting lost in a shopping center
6. Where would you most like to go?
   _____ to the zoo
   _____ to the planetarium
   _____ to a horror movie
   _____ to the library
7. Which would you most like to have?
   _____ one best friend
   _____ many friends
   _____ two or three good friends
8. Which would be easiest for you to do with your older brother or sister?
   _____ borrow money from him/her
   _____ go out with him/her
   _____ talk to him/her about a problem
9. What should an allowance be used for?
   _____ saving for something you want
   _____ spending on whatever you want at the moment
   _____ buying presents for others
10. What would you do if you saw your best friend steal some candy from a store?
    _____ report him
    _____ pretend you didn't see
    _____ ask him to share it with you
11. Which do you like best for dessert?
    _____ cake
    _____ pie
    _____ fruit salad
    _____ ice cream

12. Which would you rather do on a Saturday morning?

_____ sleep late

_____ play with a friend

_____ watch TV

13. Which would you least like to do?

_____ move to a new school

_____ lose your wallet

_____ break a leg

14. Which would you rather be?

_____ a fireman/woman

_____ a policeman/woman

_____ a mailman/woman

15. Which of these would you most like to have as your neighbor?

_____ a boy or girl three years younger than you who owns a pony

_____ a family with a swimming pool

_____ a new boy or girl your age

16. Which of these would you most like to see in your neighborhood?

_____ a house being painted

_____ a house being torn down

_____ a house being built

17. Which of these would you most like to see in your neighborhood?

_____ an ice-cream wagon

_____ a parade

_____ a bookmobile

18. Which of these would you want most as a neighbor?

_____ a teacher

_____ a circus clown

_____ a physician

19. Which of these would you want most as a neighbor?

_____ a boy your age

_____ a girl your age

_____ a childless couple with lots of nice pets they let you play with

20. Which of these would you want most as a neighbor?

_____ a young blind person

_____ a young crippled person

_____ an old person

21. Which would make you most uneasy?

_____ a thunderstorm

_____ a new baby-sitter

_____ going to bed alone in the dark

22. With whom would you rather spend your vacation?

_____ a friend

_____ a teacher

_____ your family

23. Which do you least like to do?

_____ get up in the morning

_____ go to bed at night

_____ keep your room neat

_____ take naps

24. Which do you like best in school?

_____ reading

_____ arithmetic

_____ spelling

25. Which would you prefer to do?

_____ do better in reading

_____ make a new friend

_____ go on a long vacation

26. Which do you like best in school?

_____ art

_____ music

_____ gym

27. If you had to go on a long trip, how would you rather travel?

_____ by train

_____ by plane

_____ by ship

28. Which chore would you rather do?

_____ wash dishes

_____ dust the furniture

_____ take the garbage out

29. Which would you rather play?

_____ piano

_____ drums

_____ violin

30. What would you do if someone hit you?

_____ tell the teacher

_____ hit him/her back

_____ walk away

31. Which would be hardest for you to do?

_____ show a bad paper to your parents

_____ walk away from a fight

_____ wait your turn when you have something exciting to say

32. Which would be hardest for you to do?

_____ move to a new school

_____ meet a new person

_____ dance with a girl/boy

33. Which would you least like to do?

_____ go to a birthday party without a gift

_____ go to a Halloween party without a costume

_____ go to a party with a torn dress/trousers

34. Which would you least like to do?

_____ go into a dark room

_____ slide down a very high slide

_____ ride a bicycle on a busy street

35. When playing house, would you rather be the

_____ mother

_____ father

_____ baby

36. Where would you like to spend your vacation?

_____ at the shore

_____ in the mountains

_____ at your grandparents' house

37. Which would you rather be?

_____ a kitten

_____ a kangaroo

_____ a lion

38. Which would you rather do?

_____ play in the snow

_____ swim in a pool

_____ swim in the ocean

39. What kind of person do you least like to sit next to? Someone who

_____ talks a lot

_____ looks at your paper

_____ can't sit still

40. What would you do if a bully bothered you on your way home from school?

_____ tell your parents

_____ tell him you are not afraid of him

_____ take a different way home

41. Which animal would you like to be?

_____ tiger

_____ monkey

_____ snake

42. How would you rather have your parent punish you?

_____ by spanking you

_____ by taking away your favorite game or toy

_____ by talking sternly to you

43. Which would you rather explore?

_____ a tree

_____ a mountain

_____ a river

44. Which would you hate most?

_____ getting a spanking

_____ going to the doctor for a shot

_____ losing a $5 bill

45. What would you least like to do?

_____ sit near someone who looks dirty

_____ sit near someone who talks a lot

_____ sit near someone who teases you

46. How would you spend $10?

_____ buy a game

_____ go to the movies

_____ treat the gang

47. Which is the most difficult for you to do?

_____ eat something you really dislike

_____ do a report

_____ clean up your bedroom

48. Which school job do you like best?

_____ being a messenger

_____ cleaning blackboards

_____ being desk inspector

49. Where would you prefer to sit?

_____ near the window

_____ near the door

_____ in the front of the room

50. Which would be hardest for you?

_____ to admit you told a lie

_____ to tell someone you broke his window

_____ to admit you cheated

51. What do you like to do best?

_____ play games

_____ read a book

_____ play outside

52. What would you do if someone took your favorite toy?

_____ hit him/her

_____ yell at him/her

_____ nothing

_____ tell him/her how it made you feel

53. Which color do you like best?

_____ red

_____ green

_____ blue

54. With whom would you like most to play?

_____ with a boy

_____ with a girl

_____ alone

55. What is hardest for you to do?

_____ be quiet

_____ talk in front of the group

_____ talk to the teacher

56. Which animal would you prefer to be?

_____ an ant

_____ a beaver

_____ a donkey

57. If you were in an accident, which injury would upset you most?

_____ two broken legs

_____ temporary loss of hearing

_____ temporary loss of eyesight

58. If you could be any person, who would you be?

_____ president of the United States

_____ top athlete in the country

_____ most popular movie star in the country

59. If you were to be born with a great gift, which would you prefer?

_____ a beautiful singing voice

_____ great artistic ability

_____ skill with your hands

60. What makes you happiest?

_____ getting all *A*s and *B*s on your report card

_____ taking a special trip with the gang

_____ having a week off from school

61. What makes you most angry?

_____ a teacher who treats you without respect

_____ a friend who won't listen to your side of an argument

_____ a brother/sister who tattles on you continuously

62. Which is most important?

_____ to work hard for your future

_____ to love others

_____ to really know yourself

63. Which would you prefer to have?

_____ good health

_____ a spouse or partner who loves you

_____ a well paid, high prestige job

64. Which is worst?

_____ to be punished by the teacher

_____ to have friends make fun of you

_____ to get bad grades on your report card

65. Which would you prefer to marry?

_____ a rich person

_____ a happy person

_____ a famous person

66. Which song do you like best? (write in the choices)

_____ _____

_____ _____

_____ _____

67. Which picture makes you happiest? (write in the choices)

_____ _____

_____ _____

_____ _____

68. Which story do you like best? (write in the choices)

_____ _____

_____ _____

_____ _____

Either/or Forced Choice

▸ PURPOSE

This exercise compels us to make a decision between two competing alternatives. "What characteristics do I identify with more—this or that?" In making your choices you must examine your feelings, your self-concept, and your values.

▸ PROCEDURE

For each of the forced-choice questions that follow, answer by writing your preference or choice in the blank space in front of the question. To use the strategy in a family or group setting, the leader asks people to move the furniture so that there is a wide path from one side of the room to the other. Then he or she asks an either/or question, like: "Which do you identify with more, an Escort or a Cadillac?" By pointing or by actually posting the choice words on the two sides of the room the leader indicates that those who identify more with Escorts are to go to the one side and those who identify more with Cadillacs are to go to the other. Each person then finds a partner on the side he or she has chosen and discusses the reasons for his or her choice. Discussion can be limited to two minutes or so.

Everyone then returns to the center of the room. The leader gives another either/or forced choice and people again choose between the two alternatives by moving to the appropriate side of the room.

This may be repeated with several questions. People should be instructed to find a new partner each time.

This is an excellent introductory exercise for a new group.

► EITHER/OR FORCED-CHOICE QUESTIONS

ARE YOU

_____   **1.** More of a saver or a spender?
_____   **2.** More like New York City or Colorado?
_____   **3.** More of a loner or a grouper?
_____   **4.** More like a rose or a daisy?
_____   **5.** More like breakfast or dinner?
_____   **6.** More like summer or winter?

► ADDITIONAL EXAMPLES

ARE YOU

_____   **1.** More like a teacher or a student?
_____   **2.** More yes or no?
_____   **3.** More here or there?
_____   **4.** More political or apolitical?
_____   **5.** More religious or irreligious?
_____   **6.** More like the country or the city?
_____   **7.** More like the present or the future?

_____ **8.** More of a leader or a follower?

_____ **9.** More physical or mental?

_____ **10.** More of an arguer or an agree-er?

_____ **11.** More intuitive or rational?

_____ **12.** More establishment or antiestablishment?

_____ **13.** More like a tortoise or a hare?

_____ **14.** More likely to walk on thin ice or to tiptoe through the tulips?

_____ **15.** More like patent leather or suede?

_____ **16.** More like a paddle or a Ping-Pong ball?

_____ **17.** More like a word processor or a quill pen?

_____ **18.** More like a falling star or a beacon light on a mountain?

_____ **19.** More like a rock band or a baroque string quartet?

_____ **20.** More like a clothesline or a kite string?

_____ **21.** More like a NO TRESPASSING sign or a PUBLIC FISHING sign?

_____ **22.** More like a flyswatter or flypaper?

_____ **23.** More like a roller skate or a pogo stick?

_____ **24.** More like a file cabinet or a liquor chest?

_____ **25.** More like a motorcycle or a tandem bicycle?

_____ **26.** More like a gourmet or a McDonald's fan?

_____ **27.** More like a bubbling brook or a placid lake?

_____ **28.** More like a screened porch or a picture window?

_____ **29.** More like a mountain or a valley?

_____ **30.** More like "A stitch in time" or "Better late than never"?

Forced-Choice Ladder

► PURPOSE

The Forced-Choice Ladder serves the same purpose as
Rank Order (Strategy Number 4, page 42) in that people
must make choices from among competing alternatives.
However, it is a much more complex strategy, with many
more items. It requires considerable thought in weighing
the relative importance of alternatives and their consequences. This strategy is also a surefire way of getting a
group immersed in a heated, though usually friendly,
discussion on issues and values.

► PROCEDURE

On a sheet of paper construct a forced-choice ladder, with
eight to sixteen steps, depending upon the number of
items in the ladder selected from the forced-choice ladder
suggestions on page 74 (see figure below). Then read each
statement in the ladder and write a key word or two from
each on one of the steps of the ladder to reflect the strength
of your feelings, pro or con, about the statements.

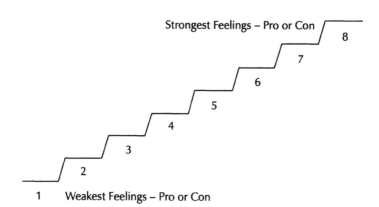

Strongest Feelings – Pro or Con

8
7
6
5
4
3
2
1   Weakest Feelings – Pro or Con

To use in a family or group setting, the leader selects a ladder and then presents the series of statements, situations, or alternatives by reading each one aloud to the family or group. Following the reading of each item, people are to write key words from the item on one of the steps of the ladder according to the strength of the feelings, pro or con, about that item. The leader explains that the ladder measures the intensity of their feelings only. It does not matter for this exercise whether the feelings are for or against. What matters is how strong the feelings are.

Sample items for a twelve-step forced-choice ladder are given on page 74.

People may cross out, draw arrows, or make changes as new items are presented. At the end, they have a few minutes to make their final arrangements.

After all the items have been read by the leader and ranked by the family or group member, people are divided into small groups of three or four to compare and discuss their responses.

We have found it to be more effective to present the statements, situations, or stories verbally, one at a time, rather than copying them or presenting them to people all at once.

An interesting and graphic extension of the forced-choice game is to have the people stand on a ladder marked on the floor to show where they have ranked certain items. This should be done after the usual procedure of ranking individually has been completed. For this purpose the ladder may be drawn with chalk, or the leader may place sheets of 8½ x 11-inch paper numbered consecutively on the floor. The leader then calls out the key words of the items one by one, and individuals are to go and stand on the number corresponding to where they placed the item on their own papers. People literally see where others "stand" on each issue.

▶ SAMPLE FORCED-CHOICE QUESTIONS

1. This is a man who is constantly stressing law and order. He is concerned about the violence and lawbreaking going on in our society. He is a building contractor. Frequently, when he gets parking tickets for his dump trucks he has them "fixed." Occasionally he does special favors for the building inspectors who inspect his work. (Key words: Law and order)

NOTE: Think about how strongly you feel, pro or con, about the man in this situation, and put the words *Law and order* on one of the steps of the ladder. Don't put the items you feel positively about toward one end and the ones that generate negative feelings toward the other. In this exercise you are to rank the items according to the strength of your feelings, regardless of whether they are positive or negative.

2. A woman believes that environmental awareness is crucial in the development of young minds. She often brings young people into the woods to experience nature. Along the way, she litters the trail with cigarette butts and an occasional soda pop can tab. (Environmental activist)

3. A high school home economics teacher is considered by everyone to be a fine teacher. She is trusted by the students. They can always turn to her. She knows that some of her students are engaging in premarital sex. She is concerned about this and gets prescriptions for birth control pills for some of her students. (Home ec teacher)

4. A high school coach is constantly scolding his gym classes because they do not exercise enough. Yet he parks his car as close as possible to the school so that he doesn't have to walk far. (The coach)

5. A man who has two children is very much concerned about the population explosion. His wife wants more children, but he doesn't. He goes to the doctor and has a vasectomy without consulting his wife. (Population explosion)

6. This man talks a great deal about how important it is for children to have a healthy emotional development. He seems to be permissive in his attitude toward children. One day he comes home and finds his three-year-old son playing with his genitals. He scolds the boy and hands him a large ball to play with instead. (Concerned father)

7. A woman believes that we should have complete freedom of personal choice. She feels that she should be able to swim where she pleases and with whom she pleases. She builds a pool and operates a segregated swim club that keeps out blacks. (Swim club)

8. A man cheats on his income tax each year, but donates all the money he saves by doing this to his church. This money is in addition to his regular contributions. (Income tax)

9. A woman was very upset about the commercialization of Christmas. She tried to convince all the aunts and uncles to agree not to send Christmas gifts to their nieces and nephews. (Worried aunt)

10. An elementary school teacher sets high standards for her pupils' performance. Many of her students place very high on national tests. Most parents want their children to be in her class. She uses fear to motivate the students, and every morning about three or four of her students feel sick to their stomachs and do not wish to go to school. (High standards)

11. A blue-collar worker's son comes home from college and criticizes his father for working in a factory that is supplying metal parts for nuclear missiles and submarines. The father tells his son to shut up and points out that the money he earns in the factory is sending the punk through college. (Blue-collar worker)

12. A boy has graduated from high school and is going off to college. Before he leaves, his mother asks him to promise not to get involved in any political marches, protests, demonstrations, or to sign any petitions because anything like that could hurt his chances in the future. She reminds him that she and his father have made great sacrifices for him and they love him a great deal. (Protective mother)

▸ ADDITIONAL SUGGESTIONS

1. A young boy tries to get even with the neighborhood grouch. On Halloween he fills a quart milk bottle with urine and leans it, without a lid, against her door. He rings the doorbell and runs. When she opens the door the urine goes all over her wall-to-wall carpet. (Halloween prank)

2. The neighborhood grouch wants to get even with the prankster. She has prepared one apple with a nail in it. She plans to give it to the boy who ruined her carpet. (Neighborhood grouch)

3. A man reports his neighbor to the Internal Revenue Service because he heard him mention at a party that he put something over on the government on his income tax. (Income tax)

4. A vice principal of a junior high school is very strict about the dress code. Any girl who comes to school in a very short dress must kneel before him. If her skirt does not touch the ground, she must go home immediately and change to more appropriate clothes. (Vice principal)

5. A college student is selling pot in the local high school to pay for his tuition. (Pot pusher)

6. A junior high school student uses a knife to scare elementary school children into paying him protection money. (Shakedown)

7. A woman comes out to her car in winter just after an ice storm. The windows are all covered with ice. She clears a tiny hole in the windshield and drives off. (Ice storm)

8. An elementary school teacher is very strict about students running in the halls. During every break he goes into the teachers' room for a cigarette. (Halls)

9. Two men get their kicks on Saturday night by going down to Greenwich Village and harassing homosexuals. (Greenwich Village)

10. A big industrialist tells his plant manager to arrange it so their smokestacks don't pollute during the day. "Save it up and let it out only at night until this ecology stuff dies down." (Pollution)

11. A Little League coach teaches his charges how to cheat without getting caught by the umpire. (Coach)

12. A man lets himself get talked into buying a vinyl hard-topped convertible. He then has to get air conditioning because the black top makes the car unbearably hot, and then he must get a bigger engine in order to run the air conditioner. (New car)

▸ **VARIATIONS**

It is possible sometimes to change the basis for evaluation by changing the ratings at the two ends of the ladder. For the following items, the top of the ladder should be marked: "The person I'd most like to be like," and the bottom of the ladder: "The person I'd least like to be like." Rank the items accordingly.

1. A rich man who gives generously to all causes, including the Nazi Party. (Charity)

2. A star athlete, always the first to come for practice and the last to leave. Some people worry that she may burn herself out young. (Athlete)

3. A teacher who is friendly with all his students. He dresses like them and goes out socially with them. (Friendly)

4. A woman with steady, directed determination begins a new career, making constructive changes in her family and society. (Career woman)

5. An ecologist who won't let his family use any paper products. (Paper)

6. A devoted husband who sends flowers on all anniversaries and birthdays and never expects any presents himself. (Flowers)

7. A college student who lends his tuition money to a friend who has to obtain an abortion. (Abortion)

8. A student who witnessed a friend taking money from another friend's wallet, tells neither friend, but replaces the money himself. (Wallet)

9. Parents who run their family with complete democracy—one person, one vote. Even the three-year-old has a vote on where to go for their vacation. (Vote)

10. A white couple who, instead of having their own babies, adopt two black babies. (Babies)

11. A cop who turns her own son in for smoking pot. (Incorruptible)

12. A student who is very popular because he makes everyone feel good. He never expresses his own feelings or opinions if they are controversial. (Popular)

13. A pilot has to make a forced landing and crashes into the woods instead of coming down on the elementary school playground because she saw two kids playing. (Airplane)

14. A teacher who always looks the other way when kids cheat on tests he is proctoring. (Tests)

15. A mother who has only one dress of her own because all her money goes for her three daughters to dress as knockouts in high school. (Dress)

16. A junior high kid who cooks dinner two nights a week for two old invalids in his apartment building. (Cook)

For the forced-choice ladder items that follow, the top of the ladder should be marked: "Most objectionable person," and the bottom of the ladder: "Least objectionable person."*

1. **Bother Bug**—Constantly interrupts the class by talking to the teacher and bothering other children.
2. **Back Talker**—Talks back to his mother.
3. **Cheater**—Cheats in a game.
4. **Litterbug**—Drops trash on the sidewalk.
5. **Borrower**—Borrows a pencil and does not return it.
6. **Bully**—Beats up a younger child.
7. **Shoplifter**—Steals candy from a store.
8. **Firebug**—Sets fire to a building.
9. **Smoker**—Smokes cigarettes.
10. **Ratter**—Rats on a friend.
11. **Chewer**—Puts gum on the seat of a chair.
12. **Vandalizer**—Deliberately throws rocks through windows in the school.

*Thanks to Richard Davis for this and the next two sets of items.

In the next set of items for a forced-choice ladder, consider and rate how strongly you feel about issues of national concern today. Mark the top of the ladder: "Strongest feelings—pro or con," and the bottom of the ladder: "Weakest feelings—pro or con."

1. **Health Care**—Improving the country's health care system.
2. **Drugs**—Developing programs to combat drug abuse.
3. **Gender Equality**—Men and women having similar opportunities for education and employment.
4. **Budget**—Balancing the federal budget.
5. **Campaign Finance**—Reducing the influence of special interest groups in politics.
6. **Law**—Increasing respect for the law.
7. **Environment**—Controlling pollution and protecting natural resources.
8. **Sex**—The role sex plays in popular culture and society.
9. **Education**—Improving the schools.
10. **Family Values**—Strengthening the family for the benefit of family members and society.
11. **Religion**—The role of religion in everyday life and society.
12. **Employment**—Insuring more jobs and job security.

For the following forced-choice ladder, rank each item according to: Strongest feelings—pro or con—or weakest feelings—pro or con.

1. **Counterspy**—A person who accepts a government job to kill a person who is also in espionage.

2. **Doctor**—A doctor who prescribes name-brand drugs of a company in which he has been given stock by the salesman.

3. **Gambler**—A parent who plays the horses and neglects the needs of the family.

4. **Sex**—A person who satisfies his/her sex needs without marriage.

5. **Competitor**—A person who always plays to win.

6. **Fraud**—The president of a firm that purchases spoiled or poor cuts of meat to be sold to poor, unsuspecting, poorly educated people.

7. **Hit-Run Driver**—A driver who is going very fast to get to a business appointment. A child darts out between cars and is hit. The driver panics and keeps on going, leaving the injured child lying in the street.

8. **Gossip**—A person who just can't keep a confidence and often spreads malicious, false information.

9. **Cheat**—The manager tells the checker in a supermarket to overcharge each customer two cents per item to make up for the shoplifting and food eating that goes on in the store.

10. **National Guardsman**—On guard duty at a college campus a National Guardsman is harrassed by rock-throwing students and shoots at them.

11. **Two-Faced**—A person who talks about how great integration is but wouldn't want to live next door to a black.

12. **Feminist**—A woman who believes strongly in gaining equal power and recognition—always pays her own way when with a man.

13. **Hard Hat**—A person who uses an axe handle as

fists to knock some sense into the heads of political demonstrators.

14. **Informant**—A neighbor who calls the police because she suspects the teenager across the street is using pot.

15. **Prankster**—A practical joker who ridicules people's weaknesses.

16. **Withdrawer**—A person who witnesses a violent crime but doesn't want to get involved.

Values Geography

► **PURPOSE**

Values Geography can help us recognize and clarify such life decisions as: "Where do I want to live?" "What kind of environment do I need?"

► **PROCEDURE**

Find a map, draw a map, or imagine that the room you are in represents a map of the city, state, nation, or world, depending upon which questions you select from those which follow. Then, for each question selected, mark the location on the map or in the room to answer that question.

To use in a family or group setting, the leader asks people to move to the center of the room and imagine that the room represents a map of the United States (city, world, and so on—see variations). He or she then asks them a series of values-geography questions. Following each question, the people are to move to a location on the "map." For example, the leader might ask, "Where were you born?" People who were born in the Midwest would move to the center of the room, and so on. There they are instructed to find partners and to share for two minutes something about why they are there.

The leader might then ask some clarifying questions, such as:

What are your feelings about being born there?
Are you proud to be associated with that part of the country?
What was the nicest thing about the place?
Is that a place where you would like to have your children be born and raised?

Then the leader asks another question like the ones below. Again, people mark their answers on their maps or move to that part of the map, find partners, and discuss why they are there.

▶ VALUES-GEOGRAPHY QUESTIONS

1. Where is a place you would like to vacation for a week? (What would you do there?)
2. Where is a place you would like to live for a year?
3. Where would you least like to live or visit?
4. If you had to choose a place to retire and money were no problem, where would you go?
5. Where would you choose to go to college? Relocate?
6. Where is a place that something important in your life happened?
7. Where is a place, more than a hundred miles away, that a special friend or relative lives? (What's special about that person?)
8. Where is the most beautiful place?

9. Where is a place you had a religious or spiritual experience?
10. Where did you have one of your most important learning experiences?

Any number of new questions can be created and substituted for these.

▶ **VARIATIONS**

Younger children may not have had the travel experience or the geographical perspective to enable them to become involved in a map of an entire country. In that case, it helps to reduce the scope of the map. For example:

1. Turn the floor of the room into a map of the city or town. Show them where some landmarks are—the schools, the river, downtown, and so on.
2. Diagram the school.
3. For older children and adolescents, the scale can be expanded—Europe, Asia, Western or Eastern Hemisphere, the world, and so on.
4. Physical maps can be created by placing strips of masking tape on the floor to represent the borders of countries, states, and so on. This can help children learn to visualize maps, compare the relative size of states, and so on.
5. People can be given a photocopied map of the United States, city, world, and so on, and then asked to code the map to indicate, for instance, where they were born by placing the word *born* on the map. Each question would have a key word to be written on the maps—*vacation, live, retire,* and so on.

Values Continuum

▶ PURPOSE

The Values Continuum serves to open up the range of alternatives possible on any given issue. As a result we begin to realize that on many issues there are various shades of gray; we are more likely to move away from the either/or, black/white thinking that often occurs when controversial issues are raised. In a family or group setting, the Values Continuum also encourages us to make public affirmations of our opinions and beliefs.

▶ PROCEDURE

Select one or more of the values continuums that follow and mark your position on each continuum with an X. Then, briefly in writing, note your reasons for selecting this position.

To use in a family or group setting, the leader draws a long line on a big piece of paper and lists two polar positions on the issue selected. For example, one end position might be: "Complete government control over economic affairs," and the other end position might be: "Absolutely no government control over the economic system." The two positions are placed on the opposite ends of the line, as shown below.

! _____ !

COMPLETE CONTROL   NO CONTROL

The leader then marks a series of points along the continuum, saying, "Between these end points there are numerous other positions. I am going to whip around the room and ask each of you to tell me where *you* stand on this issue. Briefly describe your position, without giving your reasons for holding that position. Tell me how much control you think is desirable and indicate where along the continuum you want to place yourself. Later you can share your reasons for your position. You may pass if you wish."

The leader goes around the room or calls on volunteers. People place their names on the line and briefly tell what their placement stands for. The leader may then put his or her own name on the line and explain what his or her position is.

By now every person in the room has considered the issue and freewheeling discussion can easily begin.

► **VARIATIONS**

The continuum can be a real or an imaginary line right down the center of the room. People can actually place themselves on the line and negotiate with the others to their right and left to ascertain the correctness of their position. Individuals who are at the two opposite ends might profit from discussing their differences.

Or the leader can post a very long continuum on the

wall, identifying the issue and the end positions. A marking pen and masking tape are made available. People write in their names somewhere along the line whenever they wish. As people see the continuum develop and have time to reflect on their choice, they may want to change their position. All they have to do is put masking tape over their name and write it in again at a new position. The same procedure can be followed now and then with new issues.

Sometimes people tend toward compulsive moderation. They place themselves right in the middle, thereby hoping to avoid conflict or the need to think critically. One thing you can do if this occurs frequently is to simply eliminate the middle of the continuum.

▶ ADDITIONAL SUGGESTIONS

1. What should the U.S. attitude be on involvement with other countries?

! _____ !

HELP EVERY	HELP NO
COUNTRY EVEN IF	COUNTRY—COMPLETE
NOT ASKED TO DO SO	ISOLATION

2. How far would you go to be popular with your group?

! _____ !

DO ANYTHING,	DO NOTHING AT ALL
INCLUDING RISKING	
SAFETY	

3. How much personal freedom do you have?

! _____ !

ALL DECISIONS ARE	COMPLETE FREEDOM
MADE FOR YOU	TO CHOOSE FOR
	YOURSELF

4. How much freedom do you want?

! _____ !

ALL DECISIONS TO BE   COMPLETE FREEDOM
MADE FOR YOU   TO CHOOSE FOR
                                       YOURSELF

5. How active are you in generating school (or family, team, and so on) spirit?

! _____ !

EARMUFF ELLIE   CHEERLEADER
                                       CHARLENE

(Earmuff Ellie has so little school spirit that if she is forced to go to a pep assembly or game, she wears earmuffs and blinders and sits on her hands. Cheerleader Charlene gets so carried away with keeping the student body whipped into a frenzy that she doesn't know which team is winning and sometimes cheers when the other team makes a point.)

6. How do you feel about what you wear?

! _____ !

HOLEY   WRINKLE-FREE
HAROLD—ALWAYS   WALT—IS SO
HAS HOLES IN HIS   METICULOUS HE
CLOTHES EVEN WHEN   EVEN IRONS HIS
THEY'RE NEW   UNDERWEAR
                                       CAREFULLY

7. How do you feel about arguing or fighting?

! _____ !

JET-FLIGHT   SCARFACE STU—JUST
JERRY—JERRY   LOOK AT STU
TAKES OFF IN THE   CROSSWISE AND
OPPOSITE DIRECTION   YOU'LL FIND HIS FIST
AT THE SIGN OF ANY   IN YOUR FACE
DISPUTE

8. How are you at decision making?

! _____ !

COMPLETELY UNABLE	DON'T WASTE A
TO MAKE DECISIONS,	SECOND THINKING;
EVEN ABOUT WHAT	MAKE LIGHTNING-
TO WEAR	FAST DECISIONS
	ABOUT EVERYTHING

9. How do you feel about competition?

! _____ !

AVOID ANY SITUATION	WILL TRAMPLE
WHERE THERE IS A	ANYONE FOR THE
CHANCE TO WIN OR	CHANCE TO WIN, AND
LOSE	USE ANY MEANS

10. How much do you want from the family?

! _____ !

COMPLETE	COMPLETE
DEPENDENCE ON	INDIFFERENCE TO
FAMILY; NO OUTSIDE	FAMILY; WOULD
INTERESTS, FRIENDS,	RATHER BE RID OF
AND SO ON	THEM

11. How do you feel about school?

! _____ !

DYNAMITE	STOWAWAY
DAN—STUDENTS	STEVE—LOVES
WOULD BE BETTER	SCHOOL SO MUCH
OFF IF THE SCHOOL	THE JANITOR HAS TO
WERE BLOWN TO BITS	DRIVE HIM OUT OF
	THE SCHOOL EACH
	NIGHT BEFORE
	LOCKING UP

12. How much do you talk to other people?

! _____ !

TIGHT-LIPPED TAMMY	BLABBER-MOUTH
	MONTY

13. What will you eat?

!_____!

PICKY PAUL   EAT-ANYTHING-AND-
                                              EVERYTHING ELOISE

14. How do you feel about divorce?

!_____!

STEADFAST   MULTIMARRYING
STELLA—UNDER NO   MARTHA—AT THE
CIRCUMSTANCES   DROP OF THE FIRST
                                              UNKIND WORD

15. What do you do with your money?

!_____!

HOARDING   HANDOUT
HANNAH—WON'T   HELEN—SPENDS IT
SPEND A PENNY   ALL OR GIVES IT ALL
                                             AWAY; NEVER HAS
                                             ENOUGH LEFT FOR
                                                 NECESSITIES

16. How do you feel about integration?

!_____!

FAVORS COMPLETE   COMPULSIVE   ACTIVELY
AND IMMEDIATE   MODERATE—FIGHTS   OPPOSED—
INTEGRATION AND   FOR OPEN HOUSING   WITHDRAWS CHILD
ENFORCED BUSING   EXCEPT IN HIS OWN   FROM PUBLIC
                       NEIGHBORHOOD   SCHOOL

17. How do you like bosses to relate to you?

!_____!

SUPER-BUDDY—LETS   COMPULSIVE   VERY STRICT AND
US DO ANYTHING   MODERATE—GIVES   PUNITIVE—BERATES
HOW WE WANT TO   INSTRUCTIONS BUT   US FOR A
                       DOESN'T REALLY   MISSPELLED MEMO
                       CARE HOW WE DO

18. How do you feel about defense?

! _____ !

PACIFIST	NUCLEAR
PETE—WANTS NO	NED—WANTS TO
MILITARY	SPEND ALL TAX
INSTALLATIONS OR	MONEY ON MAKING
WEAPONS	MORE-POWERFUL
DEVELOPMENT	BOMBS

19. What percentage of the time are you happy?

0% _____ 100%

SAD-SACK SARA	HAPPY-TIME HELEN

20. How do you feel about your job?

! _____ !

WORRYWART WILMA	COULDN'T-CARE-
	LESS CAROL

21. How much do you try to please others?

! _____ !

REBEL RALPH	APPLE-POLISHER AL

22. How do you feel about your/others' appearance?

! _____ !

INSPECTOR	INDIFFERENT
IRWIN—INSPECTS	IGOR—WOULD
TOENAILS EVERY	BARELY BLINK AN
MORNING	EYELASH IF PEOPLE
	WORE RAGS

23. How clean do you keep your room/house/office?

! _____ !

EAT-OFF-THE-FLOOR	GARBAGE-DUMP
ELLEN	GRETA

24. How do you feel about premarital sex?

! _____ !

VIRGINAL	WILD-OATS
VIRGINIA—WEARS	WINNIE—NEVER
WHITE GLOVES ON	PASSES UP AN
EVERY DATE	OPPORTUNITY

25. How would you raise your child?

! _____ !

SUPER-PERMISSIVE	SUPER-STRICT STEVE
PERRY	

26. How do you feel about conservation?

! _____ !

WILDERNESS	CONCRETE
WINNIE—THINKS 95	CORA—WOULD BE
PERCENT OF	READY TO PAVE
COUNTRY SHOULD	EVERYTHING OVER IF
REMAIN "FOREVER	IT WOULD STIMULATE
WILD," WITH 5	ECONOMIC
PERCENT FOR	DEVELOPMENT
POPULATED AREAS	

27. How many friends do you need?

! _____ !

STUCK-UP	FRIENDLY
STANLEY—ONLY ONE	FRANK—WANTS
FRIEND—HIMSELF—SENDS	EVERYONE TO BE HIS
HIMSELF VALENTINES	FRIEND; SENDS FIVE
	POUNDS OF CANDY TO
	EVERYONE HE
	KNOWS

28. How patriotic are you?

! _____ !

GRIPING GERTIE—MY	STARS-'N'-STRIPES
COUNTRY'S ALWAYS	STELLA—MY
WRONG	COUNTRY'S NEVER
	WRONG

29. How helpful are you to others?

! _____ !

NASTY
NELLIE—WOULDN'T
DO A FAVOR, EVEN
FOR HER OWN
BENEFIT

SUGAR-SWEET
SUE—ALWAYS
OFFERS HELP, EVEN
WHEN NOT WANTED

30. How do you feel about seat belts?

! _____ !

WASHY
WILLIE—WEARS
THEM ALL THE TIME,
EVEN TO WASH THE
CAR

SCISSORS SAM—CUTS
THEM OUT OF CARS
IN PARKING LOTS

31. How much do you watch TV?

! _____ !

BLURRY-EYED
BILL—NEVER TURNS
IT OFF

NO-KNOB
NED—NEVER TURNS
IT ON

32. How selective are you about TV?

! _____ !

ANYTHING THAT
HAPPENS TO BE ON

ONLY WATCHES
SPECIFIC, FAVORITE
PROGRAMS

33. What are your newspaper habits?

! _____ !

NEVER LOOK AT ONE,
NOT EVEN COMICS OR
SPORTS PAGES

READ EVERY WORD,
FROM COMICS TO
EDITORIALS

34. How sanitary are you?

! _____ !

DIRTY   GERMPROOF
DENNY—CHEWS   GERRY—WASHES
USED GUM FROM   HANDS BEFORE EACH
UNDERNEATH DESKS   BITE

35. How legible is your handwriting?

! _____ !

SCRIBBLY   CLEAR-AS-PRINT
SAM—CAN'T READ   CLARENCE—SPENDS
HIS OWN WRITING   HOURS WRITING
                                 EVERY ASSIGNMENT

36. What kind of Halloween celebrant are you?

! _____ !

MISCHIEVOUS   GOODY
MARY—ALL TRICKS,   GERTIE—WOULDN'T
EVEN AFTER TREATS   TRICK ANYONE—HAS
                                  NEVER PLAYED A
                               JOKE ON ANYONE IN
                                        HER LIFE

37. What kind of Christmas/holiday celebrant are you?

! _____ !

GIMME GARY—CARES   GIVEY
ONLY ABOUT WHAT   GLADYS—GENEROUS
HE'LL GET   TO A
                               FAULT—REFUSES TO
                                 OPEN ANY GIFTS
                                GIVEN TO HER

38. Where would you place yourself on this continuum?

! _____ !

TOTALLY   TOTALLY SPIRITUAL
MATERIALISTIC

39. What percentage of your waking hours do you like to spend alone?

0% _____ 100%

40. What percentage of your friends are a different religion from yours? What percentage are a different race?

0% _____ 100%

STRATEGY 9

Spread of Opinion*

► PURPOSE

Very often with controversial subjects, we tend to see things only in either/or, black or white terms. Along with the Values Continuum (Strategy Number 8, page 87), this strategy can be used to help us see the wide range of possible positions on any given issue. It asks you to take an even deeper look at various positions than does the values continuum.

► PROCEDURE

Select one of the controversial issues below. Identify several possible positions that can be taken on the issue.

ABORTION
POPULATION CONTROL
WELFARE
PREMARITAL SEX
LEGALIZATION OF MARIJUANA

---

*The authors learned this strategy from Louis E. Raths.

DISTRIBUTION OF WEALTH
HEALTH CARE REFORM
GRADING SYSTEMS
ENERGY
REDUCING CRIME

For example, on any of the above issues you might identify an ultraconservative stand, a conservative stand, a moderate stand, a liberal stand, a radical stand, and a revolutionary stand. Then, take one of these positions— not necessarily your own position—and write a paragraph defending this position. Repeat this until all positions are defended. Then choose your position.

To use in a family or group setting, each person chooses a position and writes a paragraph defending it. When this has been completed, each person reveals and discusses his or her position.

Sometimes after people have written in defense of an arbitrarily selected position, each person takes the stand that comes closest to his or her own real opinion and rewrites or adds to the paragraph so that it most clearly expresses his or her own viewpoint. The paragraph may be photocopied and handed out to everyone in the group.

Values Statements and Whips*

▸ **PURPOSE**

Typically, values statements and whip questions deal with one of the seven valuing processes: seeking *alternatives*, evaluating the *consequences* of alternatives, *choosing freely*, *prizing* choices or actions, *affirming* choices or actions, *acting* upon choices, and developing a *pattern* of behavior. The goal is to help you explore these seven aspects of valuing.

▸ **PROCEDURE**

Select a number of the values questions below and answer them by making or writing out a response statement for each.

To use the strategy in a family or group setting, the leader poses a question to the family or group and provides a few moments for people to think about their answers. Then the leader whips around the room, calling upon individuals to give their answers. The answers should be

---

*Thanks to Merrill Harmin for this strategy idea.

brief and to-the-point statements, although sometimes a person may want to give a little background to better explain his or her answer. Individuals may choose to pass.

▶ **SAMPLE QUESTIONS**

1. What is something you are proud of?
2. What is some issue about which you have taken a public stand recently?
3. What was a recent decision you made that involved consideration of three or more alternatives?
4. What is something you really believe in strongly?

▶ **ADDITIONAL QUESTIONS**

1. What is one thing you would change in our world? In your town? Your school? Your neighborhood?
2. What is one thing you hope your own children will not have to go through?
3. What is one thing about which you have changed your mind recently?
4. Who is one person you know who seems to have it "more together" than you? What can you borrow from his life?
5. How did you handle a recent disagreement?
6. What would you have Ralph Nader work on next?
7. What could you, personally, give to the presidential candidate of your choice?
8. What is one issue on which you have not yet formed a definite opinion?
9. Who is the fairest person you know? What is his or her secret?
10. What national issue do you get most passionate about?

11. What do you want to do about racism?
12. What is something in the news that really disturbed you lately?
13. Which local issue disturbs you?
14. Where do you want to be twenty years from now?
15. How much time do you spend worrying about nuclear warfare? AIDS?
16. Would you be willing to limit car usage in order to reduce noise and pollution?
17. What one quality do you want in a friend?
18. What is something you really want to learn how to do before you die?
19. What are two places you must see this year?
20. What would you do if you objected to a new local law?

Other questions for values whips may be found among the Public Interview questions (Strategy Number 12, page 107).

Proud Statements and Whips

▶ PURPOSE

The Proud Statement or Proud Whip is a variation of the Values Statements and Whips (Strategy Number 10, page 100). It helps you become more aware of the degree to which you are proud of your beliefs and actions, and this will encourage you to do more things in which you can take pride. This is why we have focused on it as an independent strategy.

▶ PROCEDURE

Select several of the proud statement questions and answer them by making or writing out a statement for each.

To use the strategy in a family or group setting, the leader asks family or group members to consider what they have to be proud of in relation to some specific area or issue. The leader then whips around the room, calling upon people in order. Individuals respond with the words "I'm proud of . . ." or "I'm proud that . . . ." Any person may pass if he or she chooses.

► SAMPLE QUESTIONS

1. What is something you are proud of that you can do on your own?
2. What is something you are proud of in relation to money?
3. What are you proud of that has to do with work (school)?
4. What are you proud of about your gift giving?
5. What is something you have written that you are proud of?
6. What are you proud of in relation to your family?
7. What is something you have done about the environment that you're proud of?

NOTE: We want to emphasize that the type of pride that is called for here is not the boastful or bragging kind of pride, but the pride that means "I feel really good about" or "I cherish" this aspect of life.

► ADDITIONAL QUESTIONS

(I am proud of . . . I am proud that . . .)

1. Any new skill you have learned within the last month or year.
2. Something you did that involved creativity.
3. A decision you made that required considerable thought.
4. The completion of a task that was very laborious but that you stuck out.
5. Some family tradition you are particularly proud of.
6. Something you refrained from doing about which you're proud.

7. Anything you've done for an older person.

8. A time when you said something when it would have been easier to remain silent.

9. A time when you didn't say something when it would have been easier to say something.

10. An athletic feat you did recently that you are proud of.

11. Anything you've made with your own hands.

12. A time recently when you made a shrewd purchase or got a good bargain.

13. A habit you worked to overcome and succeeded.

14. Anything you've done about increasing your repertoire of responses to a situation.

15. A time you were especially loving to someone and about which you feel proud.

16. Anything you did to resist conformity.

17. Anything you did to conform when everyone around you was resisting conformity.

18. A dangerous thing you tried and succeeded at.

19. A conversation recently in which you held nothing back but told exactly where you were at.

20. A new learning about which you feel proud.

21. A way in which you helped your family (your friend).

22. Anything you did to contribute to multicultural understanding.

23. Something you did to *live* by your religion or spiritual beliefs.

24. Anything you've done to add to the quantity of love in this world.

25. Something you've done to add to the store of beauty in this world.

26. A way in which you helped make democracy mean more than a word.

27. Anything you've done to support your stand on developing a world community, whatever your stand is.
28. Something you did for someone else that was extremely tender.
29. A funny thing you did about which you are proud.
30. A time when you were an important example for a younger person.

PROUD STATEMENTS AND WHIPS FOR YOUNGER CHILDREN

1. I am proud that on my own I can . . .
2. I am proud that I spent my allowance on . . .
3. I am proud that when I am scared I . . .
4. When I watch TV I am proud that . . .
5. I am proud that I made my friend happy by . . .
6. I was proud that even when the other kids did . . . I . . .
7. I am proud that this summer I . . .
8. Something my family has done all together this year that made me proud . . .
9. I am proud that I use my toys . . .
10. I am proud of what I did about . . .
11. I am proud when the other kids say that . . .
12. I'm proud that I made . . .
13. I'm proud that I helped keep my city clean by . . .
14. I am proud that I keep healthy by . . .
15. I'm proud that I helped make my school a happier place by . . .
16. I'm proud that my father (mother) . . .

Public Interview

▸ PURPOSE

This strategy gives you center stage in an imaginary or real setting and the opportunity to publicly affirm and explain your stand on various values issues. Later on, after the interview, you often will go over your answers in your own mind and thoughtfully consider what you have said during the interview.

▸ PROCEDURE

Imagine that you are to appear as a guest on a popular TV talk show. From the interview questions that follow, select the ones you would like the talk show host to ask you. Then formulate your answers by making notes on 3 × 5-inch cards or writing out your responses.

To use the strategy in a family or group setting, the leader asks for volunteers who would like to be interviewed publicly about some of their beliefs, feelings, and actions. The volunteer sits in a chair in front of the room, and the leader moves to the back of the room and asks the questions from there.

The leader reviews the ground rules: The leader may ask the volunteer a question about any aspect of his or her life and values. If the volunteer answers the question, he or she must answer honestly. However, the volunteer has the option of passing if he or she does not wish to answer one or more of the questions the leader poses. The volunteer can end the interview at any time by simply saying, "Thank you for the interview." In addition he or she may, at the completion of the interview, ask the leader any of the same questions that were put to him or her.

▶ INTERVIEW QUESTIONS

QUESTIONS FOR ADULTS AND OLDER ADOLESCENTS

1. Do you like to take long walks? Which place do you like to walk to the most?
2. About how much money do you plan to spend on Christmas or holiday gifts this year? Is that more or less than last year?
3. Do you watch TV much? How much?
4. What is your opinion on public welfare? (or any other political issue you may think is appropriate)
5. How many hours of sleep do you get on the average each night? What effect do you think this has on your lifestyle?
6. Do you have a personal motto you live by?
7. What is your stand on the use of birth control pills?
8. How much do you like to give to charities, causes, and so on?
9. Whom will you support in the coming election?
10. What is your stand on smoking?
11. How do you feel about the grading system (A, B, C, D, F)?

12. What do you plan on doing this (Thanksgiving, Easter, Christmas, summer) vacation?

13. What parts of nature do you love the most?

14. Have you ever made a choice that surprised everyone?

15. Do you have a role model? What is it about him/her you admire?

16. Should schools give students full birth control information? If yes, at what age?

17. What is one thing you would like to learn before you die?

18. How do you deal with unpleasant aspects of your work or school?

19. What brand of toothpaste do you use? How did you come to use that brand?

20. Who was your best friend before the best friend you now have?

21. Did you ever write a letter to the editor? What was the topic?

22. How important are engagement rings to you?

23. What are you saving money for?

24. Do you buy many audio or video recordings? What kind?

25. Are you more or less religious now than you were three years ago?

26. Have you ideas about what you would like to do five years from now? Ten years? Twenty years?

27. What possibilities for your future have you talked over with your loved ones?

28. How do you feel when you visit a hospital?

29. If you could learn a new skill, what would it be?

30. What is one thing that you hope to continue doing throughout your life?

31. Is there any particular organization or club you want to belong to? Why?

32. How do you spend your time after work/school?

33. Of all the things you do in your free time, which do you like most?

34. Which of your free-time activities do you like least?

35. What does your family usually do for Thanksgiving? Other holidays?

36. What have you done the last two Thanksgiving vacations?

37. What have you done the last two Christmas vacations?

38. What magazines do you read regularly?

39. Do you subscribe to any magazines yourself?

40. What are your favorite TV shows?

41. Have you seen any movies in the last few months that you liked?

42. Tell me in a sentence or two about a movie you saw and why you liked it.

43. What are your favorite sports?

44. What books have you read that you like?

45. Do you work on Saturdays? Sundays? Holidays?

46. What do you like best about your work? School?

47. What do you like least about your work? School?

48. If you could change some part of your job/educational program, what would it be?

49. If you were your boss/teacher, how would you manage things/teach your classes?

50. Have you a hobby that takes up a lot of your time? What is it?

51. How did you get interested in your hobby?

52. Are your friends/loved ones interested in the same hobby as you?

53. Are some of your friends/loved ones not interested in your hobby?
54. Is there a person you dislike intensely? Why?
55. Is there someone you admire intensely? Why?
56. Have you ever invented anything? What?
57. What is there about you that makes your friends/colleagues like you?
58. Is there something you want badly but can't afford right now? What?
59. Of all the people you know who have helped you, who has helped the most? How did he/she go about it?
60. What are some things you really believe in?
61. Where did you spend the best summer of your life?
62. If you could change your place of employment/school, what two things would you change?
63. What is the worst work you have done for money?
64. What do you see yourself doing when you retire?
65. Are there injustices in your community you feel need attention?
66. Do you give any money to charities? Which ones? Which ones do you object to supporting?
67. What is the most important book, movie, or play you've read or seen in the past year?
68. What one thing would you change about yourself if you could?
69. What is a difficult choice you face right now in your life?
70. Do you believe in burial, cremation, or what?
71. What is one action you've taken to make this world more beautiful?
72. Do you wear seat belts?
73. What are some of your notions of the good life?

74. Do you smoke? Do you use drugs?
75. Do you have full polio protection?
76. Are there things you would not tell even best friends? What kinds of things?
77. What is the most serious environmental concern you have today?
78. How do you feel about going steady?
79. Do you ever do things to make your parents feel good without their having asked you? What? When?
80. Did you ever steal something? When? How come?
81. Do you ever get teased? Do you ever tease others?
82. Describe the best teacher you ever had.
83. How have you enjoyed school over the years?
84. What, if anything, makes you dislike a person on sight?
85. Can you think of something that you would like to say to the group that you think might be good for them to hear?
86. Do you feel satisfied with your life?
87. What improvements would you like to make in your life?
88. What would you consider your main interests in life?
89. Describe something you have done recently to a person you dislike.
90. What do you do when you want to get out of something?
91. If you had an extra $500 given to you with no strings attached, what would you do with it?
92. Would you like to marry or remarry? Soon?
93. In your estimation, what is the value of a funeral?
94. How many children would you like to have?
95. How do you feel about interracial marriage?
96. How do you feel about homosexuality?

97. Which celebrity would you like to have for a friend?
98. What is one thing you could stop doing to help save energy?
99. What is your favorite color?
100. Are you satisfied with your height?
101. As a child, did you ever run away from home? Did you ever want to?
102. Do you think you were an obedient child?
103. What was the most frightening thing that ever happened to you?
104. Do you believe in life after death?
105. How often do you do something you regret?
106. How do you handle it when you do something you regret?
107. How do you think your boss/teacher(s) should dress at work/school?
108. What do you consider the worst thing you ever did?
109. Do you have a favorite food?
110. How often do you eat out?
111. Do you ever cook? What do you make?
112. What is one idea, skill, or article you have passed on to others this past year?
113. Who are the other people in your family?
114. Describe one of the people in your family in two sentences.
115. What present would you most like to get?
116. Do you do things spontaneously or do you think things through before doing anything?
117. Do you ever do things just because others expect you to do them that way?
118. Should people always do what they like to do?
119. How do you know when something is right or wrong?
120. Do you think a person should tell another person

about something personal and embarrassing, such as bad breath or soiled clothes?

121. If someone embarrassed you, what would you do?

122. Do you enjoy your pace of life at present? Would you like to speed it up or slow it down?

123. What do you think of the new president (governor, and so on)?

124. Do you feel the problems of pollution are being exaggerated? How about AIDS? Drugs? Crime?

125. If you could change one thing during your lifetime, what would it be?

126. Do you get enough money for your work/allowance?

127. Are you proud of being a man/woman (girl/boy)?

128. Would you tell your best friend he or she has bad breath?

129. Have you experienced death close to you?

130. Would you marry someone of another race?

131. Do you have faith in our political system?

132. Are you proud of your work habits?

133. Do you practice your religion?

134. Can you tell your friends/loved ones your personal problems?

135. How would you feel about calling your boss/teacher by his/her first name?

136. What are three things you are good at?

137. What, if any, career goals do you have?

138. Have you ever written a letter to a company complaining about a product?

139. What is one event that took place in your life that made a big difference?

140. How much TV do you watch?

141. Have you ever tried to return a product to a store because it was defective?

142. Do you feel your boss/teachers is/are fair?

143. What is something interesting people might never know about you?

144. What is your most prized possession?

145. What do you enjoy most in life?

146. Are you planning to return/go to college?

147. Are you good at getting high grades?

148. What would you do if you got too much change given to you at the checkout counter?

149. Do you think social studies books should have more about multicultural contributions to our history?

150. Have you ever signed a petition? For what?

151. Have you ever been on a motorcycle? Would you wear a helmet even if it were not the law?

152. Are you curious about trying pot? Other drugs?

153. Have you ever carried a picket sign?

154. What makes your best friend your best friend?

155. Do you know how to keep a checking account? Do you balance it or write checks until they bounce?

156. What is the one thing you want to learn how to do better?

157. Do you ever treat other friends to dinner or a movie?

158. Did you ever cheat at Monopoly?

159. Do you like to get letters? To write letters?

160. Which was your best year in school?

161. Do you think you will ever dye your hair? Are you prejudiced against women or men who do?

162. If you were driving in the country at night and you came to a red light that didn't change for some time, what would you do?

163. In what ways are you a conformist?

164. Have you ever read a book that had a deep effect on your life?

165. Did you spend any time last summer flat on your back looking for falling stars?

166. Do you think you're very materialistic?

167. What would you suggest to make this a better world? Nation? City? School?

168. Would you work actively to improve your community? School? What would you do? What have you done?

169. Are you concerned about fat or cholesterol in your diet? Do you feel good about your eating habits?

170. What are your views on acupuncture and alternative health care approaches?

QUESTIONS FOR YOUNGER CHILDREN

1. What present would you give your mother for her birthday? Your father?

2. What did you like about your summer vacation?

3. What was the scariest TV show you ever watched? Do you still watch it? Who was the advertiser? What was advertised? Will you buy the product?

4. Do you and your parents enjoy watching the same TV programs?

5. How many pairs of shoes do you have? Who bought them?

6. Do you think you will grow a beard when you grow up? Let your hair grow long? Bleach your hair?

7. Do you wish your teacher were a different kind of person? How?

8. What did you have for breakfast? What is your favorite breakfast? How often do you have this? Have you ever had a day when you could ask for anything you wanted to eat?

9. Do you know any kids who shoplift?
10. What's the fastest you have ever been driven in a car?
11. Do you get an allowance?
12. Do you go to Sunday school or religion class?
13. Do you litter? Why? Why not?
14. Why do you think your friends like you?
15. Are you a member of a Brownie troop/Cub pack?
16. Do you come promptly when you are called?
17. Are you happy that you are a boy/girl?
18. Do you feel that you do your best work all the time?
19. Would you like to be older or younger than you are now?
20. Did you go on a vacation this year?
21. Do you wish you had an older sister? Brother?
22. Is your best friend a boy or a girl?
23. Would you like to be a patrol monitor?
24. What makes you most angry?
25. Do you ever do anything to earn money?
26. What would you do if you couldn't watch TV?
27. Do you like making new friends?
28. Do you think department stores should be open on Sunday?
29. Did you ever write a love letter to a boy (or a girl)?
30. Are you expected to do certain chores around the house?
31. What is the happiest thing you can remember?
32. What is the saddest thing you can remember?
33. What wish would you make?
34. Who is your closest friend?
35. What do you like best about your closest friend?
36. What do you dislike about your closest friend?

37. Would you tell your closest friend what you don't like about him/her?

38. If you could visit anyplace in the world, where would you go?

39. Tell me three things you like to do best.

40. Tell me three things you like to do least. Rank them.

41. Have you ever been very sick?

42. Are you enjoying school?

43. What do you like to do after school?

44. Do you like being inside or outside more?

45. Do you like to walk?

46. Do you like babies? Why?

47. Is there something that you once did that you are especially proud of?

48. Do you have a special place of your own?

49. Can you tell me one nice thing about yourself?

50. Can you tell me one bad habit that you have?

51. What is your full name? Do you like it? Would you change it if you could?

52. Do you have any brothers or sisters? How do you get along?

53. Do you ever daydream? What about?

54. What do you do around the house in the way of chores?

55. Do you get an allowance? Is it fair? What do you do with it?

56. Are you rich? Do you want to get rich when you grow up?

57. How do people get rich? Why are some people poor?

58. Do you like to be teased? How does it make you feel?

59. How do you show your parents that you love them?

60. Would you like to live in the country or in the city?

61. Do you like school? Do you think you'll go to college?

62. What kind of work do you want to do when you grow up?

63. Would you like to get married? What kind of person would you choose?

64. Would you make a good husband/wife?

65. How many children do you think you'll want?

66. Do you have any friends of different religions or races?

67. Are you allowed to make a lot of your own decisions at home? About what?

68. Who decides how you should wear your hair? What clothes you should wear?

69. What's your favorite ice cream flavor?

70. Did you ever ask your parents where babies come from?

71. Would you like to be an author someday?

72. Do you have any hobbies?

73. How much time do you spend watching TV? What are your favorite TV shows?

74. How often do you go to the movies?

75. What book have you read that you liked very much?

76. Do you think you'd make a good teacher?

77. If you were a teacher, would you be strict?

78. Is there someone you dislike a lot? Why?

79. What is there about you that makes your friends like you?

80. Do you have one close friend or many friends?

81. Would you want a black person (white person, Asian person) for your neighbor?

82. Would you invite a black person (white person, Asian person) to your house for dinner?

83. Would you join the army?
84. Do you think you'll smoke someday?
85. Why do you think some people take dope?
86. What would you do if you found someone's wallet with money in it?
87. Do you have a pet?
88. Do you want a big wedding?
89. Do you like to eat sweets?
90. Do you buy or bring your lunch?
91. Have you ever stolen anything?
92. Is there something special you want for your birthday?
93. Do you ever have trouble falling asleep?
94. Did you ever cheat on a test?
95. If you could go anywhere in the world, where would you like to go?
96. Are you ever alone in the house? How often? How do you feel?
97. What time do you go to bed? Who decides?
98. Have you ever made anything? What?
99. What do you think happens to people after they die?
100. Do you have your own room at home? If not, who shares it with you?
101. Do you get an allowance? What kind? Do you have to do anything for it?
102. Do you go to Sunday school or religion class? Do you enjoy it?
103. What's fun to do with your family?
104. If you could be any age, what age would you like to be?
105. Did you go on a vacation this year? If you could go anywhere in the world you wanted to next year, where would you go?

106. Will you become a couch potato? Why?

107. Do you wish you had a larger family or a smaller family, or is your family just the right size?

108. As you look at the world around you, what is something you sometimes wonder about?

109. Do you like daytime or nighttime better?

110. What is your favorite dessert?

111. Do you like to climb trees? Ice-skate? Go to the movies?

112. Would you like to fly a plane?

113. If you could have $100 cash, what would you do with it?

114. Would you like to ask *me* any questions?

The Talk Show Host Interview

► PURPOSE

This strategy is a major variation on the Public Interview (Strategy Number 12, page 107). Its purpose is to give you a chance to think about what questions are important to ask others and, therefore, to ask yourself.

► PROCEDURE

Identify a person whom, if you could act as a TV talk show host, you would like to interview. It can be a friend or a loved one; someone who is rich, famous, or powerful; someone from the past; or a fictional character from a book, movie, or play. Select the interview questions you would like to ask him or her. Use questions from Strategy Number 12 or make up your own questions.

If the person you chose is unavailable for you to interview, write out your answers to the questions and share them with a friend or family member. If the person you chose is available and willing, sit down with him or her and actually conduct your talk show host interview.

The Family and Group Interview

► PURPOSE

This strategy, done in the family or small groups, provides individuals with an opportunity to share on a more intimate basis than in the Public Interview (Strategy Number 12, page 107) some of their personal interests, beliefs, activities, and values. It also affords individuals with the experience of interviewing each other.

► PROCEDURE

The family does this activity as a group. In a larger group setting, the leader breaks the larger group into smaller groups of four to six. One member of the family or group volunteers to be interviewed by the group. Before the interview starts, group members take a minute or two to write down any questions they would like to ask the focus person. The volunteer may also write down questions he or she would like to be asked and passes these to a group member. The questions should deal with interests, hobbies, family, friends, beliefs, hopes, goals in life, and activities. (See Strategy Number 12 for ideas, page 107.) Then the group members ask the focus person questions. The focus controls the interview by calling upon group members as he or she chooses. He or she has the option of not answering any question that is too personal or inappropriate by saying, "I pass." He or she may also question a group member about his or her purpose in asking a question before choosing to answer it. Unless there is a time limit set, the interview is over when there are no more questions or when the interviewee ends it by saying, "Thank you for your questions."

The interview is to be conducted by the following ground rules:

1. Personal information, beliefs, and values are to be shared and discussed on a voluntary basis. Please remember that there are things all of us do not wish to discuss with others at a particular moment. This feeling should be recognized and respected by all members of the group.

2. The group interview is not the place for argument or debate. Please respect each other's right to live differently, feel differently, think differently, and value differently. You may disagree with someone in the group, but try to understand his position rather than telling him he is wrong or trying to make him change.

▶ **VARIATIONS***

Rather than have one focus person, the group can start by asking one member a question, and then that person can ask another group member a question, and so on. The chain continues in this way until the group decides to stop.

---

*The authors learned these variations from Merrill Harmin.

Or one or more questions can be answered by each and all group members. This is most effective when the answers are brief (one or two sentences), thus forming a kind of "interview whip."

I Learned Statements*

▸ PURPOSE

This strategy helps us clarify and reinforce what we have learned. It crystallizes new learnings we might not have realized were taking place.

▸ PROCEDURE

As a follow-up to one or several of the strategies in this book, complete the sentence stems below. Then take a few minutes to reflect on what you have learned or discovered and how it might affect how you behave and live.

To use with a family or group, the leader prepares a chart with the following (or similar) sentence stems. The chart may be posted permanently in the room or it may be posted just when it is to be used.

I learned that I . . .	I realized that I . . .
I relearned that I . . .	I was surprised that I . . .
I noticed that I . . .	I was pleased that I . . .
I discovered that I . . .	I was displeased that I . . .

*Thanks to Jerry Weinstein for this strategy.

Right after the values activity or discussion, the leader asks individuals to think for a minute about what they have just learned or relearned about themselves or their values. Then they are to use any one of the sentence stems to share their learnings with each other.

Statements should be kept short and to the point. Focus on personal learnings rather than on general, intellectualized learnings. There is a tendency to say, "I learned that people . . ." rather than "I learned that *I*. . . ."

▸ SUGGESTION

Compile a list of I Learned Statements in writing, date it, and put it in your Values Journal (Strategy Number 17, page 130).

I Wonder Statements*

► PURPOSE

This rather simple but powerful strategy is designed to help you raise and make a note of questions that may have arisen in your mind. It provides a fruitful source of questions to encourage future learning.

► PROCEDURE

Upon completion of a values activity or discussion, complete in writing sentences beginning with "I wonder," such as:

I wonder if . . .   I wonder why . . .
I wonder how come . . .   I wonder whether . . .
I wonder about . . .   I wonder when . . .

To use in a family or group, the leader posts the above "I wonder" sentence stems and asks participants to complete them.

---

*Thanks to Joe Levin for the kernel idea in this strategy.

Then the focus goes round and round the room as individuals share or the leader calls on people to share their I Wonder Statements with each other. Anyone may pass, of course. The leader should participate, too, and might even start it off with an example or two of his or her own. There is no discussion of the questions raised since the goal is to stimulate the sense of wonder and further inquiry. Answers may come later, over time.

The Values Journal or Values Data Bank

► **PURPOSE**

The values-clarification approach encourages us to examine our own lives in the same way that the scientific method helps the scientist explore his or her area of study. The scientist collects as much information or data as he or she can about the subject, and tries to understand the data by looking for explanations and patterns. Eventually, the scientist hopes to gain control over the subject of study—whether it is atomic energy, cancer, or a new synthetic substance.

In much the same way, we who are forging our own values place ourselves under a microscope and study our own patterns of choosing, prizing, and acting. The goal of this search is to make sense out of all the data we have collected about ourselves in order to achieve direction and control over our own life and be less at the mercy of inner compulsions and external pressures.

The Values Journal, also called the Values Data Bank, provides you with a simple storage and retrieval system for the information you collect in your search for values.

► **PROCEDURE**

Keep a journal or file or a special section in a notebook for "Values." All the notes from values activities—Privacy Circles, Values Grid, I Learned Statements, and so on—go into this journal or data bank. You can also use your values journals to jot down values-related thoughts and feelings whenever they occur. In other words, like the scientist you store the information you collect about yourself in your search for values. This is to be your own private property and no one is to look at it without your permission.

From time to time, look over the data in your journal and ask yourself questions like "Are my values concerns at all different from what they were a month ago? Am I clearer now on any values issues than I was before? Are some issues more confusing? What steps do I need to take next to discover and live the values that are most important to me?"

Family or Group Values-Focus Game*

▶ **PURPOSE**

The search for values is facilitated when there is a supportive and accepting attitude in the family or group. To encourage this kind of climate, family or group members must learn to respect each other's right to hold different views and, within limits, to act in accordance with their different convictions. The Values-Focus Game is designed to help people be open to, accept, and understand different points of view even if they do not agree with them. The goal of this activity is to help you understand more effectively another person's point of view, rather than attempt to change the person's mind through attack or debate.

▶ **PROCEDURE**

To introduce the game, the leader has family or group members complete in writing several sentence stems. Two that work very well in this context are:

---

*This strategy is an adaptation of the Positive-Focus Game developed by Saville Sax.

"I feel best when I am in a group of people who . . ."
"I feel worst when I am in a group of people who . . ."

After each person has completed the unfinished sentences, the leader asks participants to arrange themselves into groups of three. Each person in the group is to have the focus—the full attention of the other two family/group members—for a period of five minutes. During this period the focus person is to talk about his or her thoughts and experiences on this topic. The group's interaction is to be governed by the following rules:

1. The Rule of Focusing. Each person is to be the focus person for a period of five minutes. Do not let the attention of the group shift from the focus person until his or her time is up or until he or she asks to stop. Maintain eye contact with the focus person at a comfortable level. Questions may be asked of the focus person if the questions do not shift the focus to another group member.

2. The Rule of Acceptance. Be warm, supportive, and accepting of the focus person. Nods, smiles, and expressions of understanding when sincerely given help communicate acceptance. If you do not agree with the focus person, do not express disagreement or negative feelings during the discussion part of the game. There will be time for this later on.

3. The Rule of Drawing Out. Attempt to understand the focus person's position, feelings, and beliefs. Ask questions that will help to clarify the reasons for the focus person's feelings. Make sure your questions do not shift the focus to yourself or reveal negative feelings that you may have about the focus person or about what he or she is saying.

Each person is provided with a copy of the rules. The leader explains them fully.

▶ SUGGESTIONS FOR USE

The Values-Focus Game can be used with almost any values activity that requires family or small group discussion. It really teaches listening. Later, the rule of focusing can be dropped, if need be, to facilitate a more free-floating discussion.

Upon completion of the game, especially the first few times, the leader may suggest that people rate themselves and each other, on a five-point scale, to assess how well they were able to follow the three rules. These ratings should then be shared and discussed in the small group with the intent of helping each other become more proficient at really listening to and understanding each other's feelings and ideas.

After the individuals have rated themselves and each other on how well they followed the three rules, time can be taken for them to react to each other's positions. They voice their agreement or disagreement and discuss their various points of view.

. . . ing Name Tags

▸ PURPOSE

This strategy asks participants to look more closely at what they value and who they are. Second, it asks them to publicly affirm these aspects of themselves. And third, it is an easy way to help a new group—no matter how large—relax a bit and begin to get acquainted.

▸ PROCEDURE

On a large (e.g., 5 × 7–inch) index card or piece of paper, write your first name with crayon or marker in large letters so it will be visible across the room. Then write five or six words ending in "ing" that tell something about who you are, e.g., piano playing, reading, fun-loving, fighting, baseball-ing, and so on. Write these words anywhere on your card on the same side as your name.

Then turn your card over and write your name again, in big letters. This time you are to write five or six words that report specific facts or statistics about yourself. This might be your address, phone number, height, number of family members, last name, eye and hair color, and so on.

When you have completed both sides, fasten the name tag to your clothes with a safety pin. Wear the name tag for a day at home or at a party. Choose which side to show the world. It is a surefire strategy for getting others to ask you about what you have written.

To use in a family or group setting, the leader asks everyone to make an -ing tag. Then everyone is to put on the name tag, get up, and mill about the room in random fashion, reading each other's name tags; looking at clothes, eyes, and faces; shaking hands; and asking questions if they feel like it. The leader can ask that this be done with or without words. Of course, he or she participates, too.

▶ VARIATIONS

Instead of -ing words, other stems that can be used are:

  -able (touchable, reasonable, breakable, lovable, improvable)
  -ful (beautiful, trustful, wasteful, angerful, spiteful)
  -ist (optimist, botanist, cyclist, realist, specialist)
  -less (careless, penniless, merciless, hopeless, errorless)

Or new words can be made up or modified, or additional information can be written on the name tags, like: a hero, a place they'd like to live, two things they think about, and so on.

Partner Risk or Sharing Trios

▸ PURPOSE

One of the seven valuing processes is self-disclosure—a willingness to openly state and to stand up for our beliefs and actions. Learning to build trust so that we can risk being open is fundamental to this process. Partner Risk or Sharing Trios is a step in this direction. We have included this strategy because most of the individual strategies and activities in this book can be used in a family or group setting by having the participants first do the individual activity, and then share, discuss, or explore it with others by doing this strategy.

▸ PROCEDURE

The leader asks participants to pick one or two partners. For five minutes (you decide the time limit), each person is to share with his or her partner(s) the high point and the low point in his/her life during the past week—that is, they are each to tell what was most satisfying in the week and what was least satisfying. When five minutes are up, each person finds a new partner or partners. The new pairs are then given a new topic to discuss for the allotted time period. (See suggested topics below.) This procedure may be repeated several times.

Following one or more discussion periods, the leader asks the participants to close their eyes and think about the following questions:

1. Were you really listened to? Did your partner really hear you? Did you listen to him/her?
2. Did you really share your feelings or did you screen them before talking about them?
3. Did you worry that you talked too much? Too little?
4. Were you mostly a "pickee" (one who was chosen by another when partners were switched) or a "picker" (one who did the choosing)? Suggestion: Next time reverse roles. If you were a "pickee," try to be a "picker." Which would you rather be?
5. Would you have added to your discussion if you had had more time?
6. Was your partner like you or quite different from you? Can you understand him/her? Do you like having a partner who is like you? Different from you?
7. Would you like your partner to have some of your experiences? Would you like to have some of his/hers?

When participants have developed acceptance and trust with each other, any of the individual strategies or activities in this book can be introduced and then shared or explored using the same partner risk or sharing trio format.

If a participant has nothing to discuss about the assigned topic, he or she may pass. If he/she wishes to substitute a topic for the one given, he/she may do so.

This is an especially good exercise to use with a new group. It builds rapport rapidly.

▶ OTHER SUGGESTED TOPICS

1. What are some things you do that you think are quite unconventional?
2. Tell about a turning point in your life.
3. Describe a time of your greatest despair.
4. Tell about the person who had the most tremendous impact upon your life.
5. Tell something about some political involvement that meant a great deal to you.
6. Tell some things that you would put in your will.
7. Describe a social evening that is the worst kind for you and tell what you do about it.
8. Tell where you stand on the topic of masturbation.
9. Share the most intense religious experience of your life.
10. Tell about a situation in which you felt very embarrassed.
11. Expound on your views about engagement rings.
12. Name three ways in which your present love relationship would be better if only the other person would . . . If only *you* would . . .
13. Tell about some of the beautiful things your family does in the realm of ritual.
14. Tell how you feel about alcohol, cigarettes, and marijuana.
15. Share a superstition you hold.
16. Disclose one area in your life where you have settled for less than you had once wanted.

17. Share some of your experiences with or feelings about death.

18. Tell in as much detail as possible what you consider the most satisfactory way to handle your burial.

19. With as much honesty as possible, tell whether you really prefer to be loved more than you can love back or to love more than you are loved back.

20. Discuss who in your family brings you the greatest sadness and why. Then share who brings you the greatest joy.

21. Share the high point of last Thanksgiving or the low point of the last Christmas or family event.

22. Share something about a hero of yours, either living or dead.

23. Share an experience you have had with a Dear John letter you have sent or received, or a letter you have written to the editor.

24. Share your opinion on premarital sex.

TOPICS FOR YOUNGER CHILDREN

1. Tell about a time when you were really needed by someone.

2. Tell about a time when you felt you were being left out of a group.

3. Tell about an adult you really respect.

4. Talk about a person who really frightened you or hurt your feelings.

5. Describe how your life might change if there were no TV.

6. Talk about some of the things that confuse you about this world.

7. Talk about your allowance—how much you get, when and how, and whether you think it's fair.

8. Tell about a time when you were deeply misunderstood.

9. Tell about a movie that touched you deeply.

10. Describe what you are sure you don't want to be like when you grow up.

11. Talk about one or more things you would like to be able to do better socially, intellectually, athletically, as a family member, as a citizen, as a friend, and so on.

12. Tell how you think this world could be better and what you could do about it.

13. Tell about the first time you felt you loved someone who was not in your family.

14. Talk about your favorite sport or game.

15. Describe your best friend, how you met, why you like him/her.

Privacy Circles

► PURPOSE

Publicly affirming our position or belief, under the appropriate circumstances, is one of the seven subprocesses of valuing. Yet it is often difficult to determine when circumstances are appropriate or inappropriate. The Privacy Circles strategy encourages you to think more about your pattern of self-disclosure and self-containment in relation to your feelings, opinions, and actions. It gives you the opportunity to find out whom you are willing to tell what. It often raises the questions: "Am I too open?" and "Am I too closed?"

► PROCEDURE

Using a full sheet of paper, draw a set of privacy circles, as pictured. Starting with the outermost circle and moving inward, each band represents less and less self-disclosure. For instance, there are some things about our lives we might be glad to let anyone, even strangers, know—our

favorite TV show, the type of hat we like to wear, our
address. Other things we might not want strangers to know
but would tell to acquaintances such as our business
associates, a neighbor, or a classmate. Still other things
we would reserve only for our friends. Then there are
thoughts and feelings we have or things we've done or do
that we would tell only our most intimate friends, perhaps
our best friend, a spouse, or family members. Finally,
there may be some aspects of our lives we would not want
to share with anyone; these are reserved only for ourselves.
(The last small circle is darkened to acknowledge that
there are some feelings or facts that we don't admit even
to ourselves.)

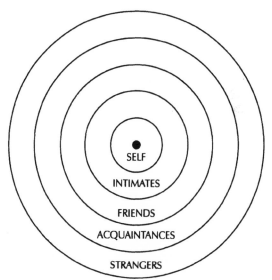

Write two things (beliefs, feelings, or actions) about
yourself in each band of the circle. In the friends' band,

for example, write two things you would tell your friends and intimates but not acquaintances or strangers, and so on for each band.

Now, go to the "To Whom Would You Tell" list that follows, and for each item selected, write the key word for the item in the band that shows to whom you would be willing to reveal your answer. Select only those items that apply to you.

NOTE: Blocks or squares may be used instead of circles. They are easier to draw and to write on.

TO WHOM WOULD YOU TELL?

1. You have a sexually transmitted disease. (Key word: *STD*)
2. Your salary. (Key word: *Salary*)
3. Whom you vote for. (Key word: *Vote*)
4. Your innermost desires. (Key word: *Desires*)
5. Your personal problems. (Key word: *Problems*)
6. Your health problems. (Key word: *Health*)
7. Your pet likes and dislikes. (Key word: *Likes*)
8. You cheat on your income tax. (Key word: *Cheat*)
9. Your income. (Key word: *Income*)
10. You have had premarital sexual relations. (Key word: *Premarital*)
11. You have considered suicide. (Key word: *Suicide*)
12. Your deeply felt religious convictions. (Key word: *Religious Beliefs*)
13. You use illegal drugs. (Key word: *Drugs*)
14. You have had an abortion. (Key word: *Abortion*)
15. Your doubts about religion. (Key word: *Religious Doubts*)

16. The major problem(s) in your marriage. (Key word: *Marriage Problems*)

17. You had a check that bounced. (Key word: *Bounced*)

18. You slapped a child. (Key word: *Slapped*)

19. The exact cost of your house. (Key word: *House*)

20. About any racist tendencies you might have. (Key word: *Racist*)

21. What you cried about the last time. (Key word: *Cried*)

22. When you experienced very profound jealousy. (Key word: *Jealousy*)

23. Your method of birth control. (Key word: *Birth Control*)

24. Your discontent with some part of your body. (Key word: *Body*)

25. About cheating or apple-polishing during your high school and college years. (Key word: *Grade-grubbing*)

26. You have had extramarital sexual experience. (Key word: *Extramarital*)

27. How much you love your family. (Key word: *Family*)

28. What you spend your money on. (Key word: *Money*)

29. The story of your first love. (Key word: *Love*)

30. What you dislike about your best friend. (Key word: *Friend*)

SOME PRIVACY CIRCLE QUESTIONS FOR YOUNG CHILDREN
(Key words are in *italics*)

1. Whom would you tell that you cried when you were left *alone*?

2. To whom would you mention that you had a *scary dream*?

3. With whom would you share that you had once *taken*

money from your dad's dresser or from your mother's pocketbook?

4. To whom would you say that you are really *good at something*—like playing first base, jumping rope, or some other skill like that?

5. To whom would you say that you are really *bad at something*, like ice-skating, baseball, math, and so on?

6. To whom would you admit that there is a *superstition* that you have?

7. Which people would you tell exactly what your *favorite meal* is?

8. Whom would you tell that you once saw something you think you *shouldn't have seen*?

9. Whom would you tell that you once did something *mean* to an animal?

10. Whom would you tell the name of your *best friend*?

22

Risk Ratio
or Force-Field Analysis

► **PURPOSE**

This activity, like Privacy Circles (Strategy Number 21, page 142), is intended to help you determine what are the proper circumstances for publicly affirming your ideas, feelings, and actions. There are times when it would be suicidal or counterproductive to make public affirmations of our values. Sometimes such affirmations would make it more difficult to work for other values we hold. Yet, sometimes not to affirm our position is nothing other than cowardice or taking the easy way out. How can we tell the difference?

> "If I tell my colleagues what I really think about issue number 1, I may be ostracized, and then I lose my power to influence positive changes on issues 2, 3, and 4. Is it worth the risk?"

> "I don't want to do what my friends do every Saturday night. Should I tell them and risk losing my membership in this group?"

> "I'd like to tell my husband what bothers me about something

he does, but I'm scared he'll get mad at me or that it will mean the end of our relationship. Is it worth the risk?"

"I'd like to tell my boss what I think of her methods, but I might get fired. Is it worth the risk?"

This strategy uses the popular Force-Field Analysis to evaluate the risks in making a public affirmation.

▶ PROCEDURE

Write on the top of a piece of paper an opinion or feeling you have that you would like to affirm—to your community, to your family, to your friends. It should be an opinion or feeling that you would have some difficulty expressing—that involves some risk.

Now, draw a line down the middle of the paper. On the left-hand side of the paper list all the advantages or possible benefits to be gained if an affirmation were made. On the right-hand side list all the disadvantages, costs, or risks that might result if an affirmation were made. Then, after comparing the list of benefits against the list of costs, write at the bottom of the paper whether you think the risk is worth taking and, if it is, whether or not you plan on taking any action at this point.

NOTE: A helpful technique for comparing the costs against the benefits is to look for listings on either side that have equal weight and would cancel each other out. Or find two costs that cancel out one of the benefits. As listings are canceled a line should be drawn through them. Finally, you will be left with more items on one side of your list than on the other. This can help you in making a decision.

Each advantage and each risk also can be given a

numerical value on a scale from one to ten. Thus a ratio of the advantages over the risks can be derived. A ratio greater than one would indicate the risk is worth taking. Conversely, a ratio of less than one would indicate the risk is not worth taking. It should be pointed out, however, that since the point value given each advantage or risk is entirely subjective, there is nothing objectively accurate about this procedure. Its value is in helping you measure your own feelings about the pros and cons of the dilemma.

The use of the Force-Field Analysis, which stems from the work of Kurt Lewin, is not limited to the issue of public affirmation. When you are considering any action that has both advantages and disadvantages, the Force-Field Analysis can be used.

The Removing Barriers to Action Strategy (Number 27, page 162) also fits in well here as a way of helping you reduce the risks of restraining forces, thus making the action more clearly advantageous.

Alternatives Search

▶ PURPOSE

When was the last time you made a choice from among more than three alternatives? This is a crucial question in the search for values, for much of the time we make our decisions and live our lives without looking at all the possible alternatives.

This activity is designed to provide you with practice in searching for alternatives. It deals with general values issues and life situations. For alternatives in specific situations that demand action, see Alternative Action Search (Strategy Number 24, page 153).

▶ PROCEDURE

Choose a values issue or life problem you are facing or one from the list provided.

Now brainstorm (Strategy Number 25, page 157) as many alternatives to the problem as you can think of in three to five minutes or a little longer.

Write down your suggested alternatives on the following chart and check the appropriate columns. This may encourage you to consider each alternative more carefully.

ALTERNATIVE	I'LL TRY IT.	I'LL CONSIDER IT.	I WON'T TRY IT.
1.			
2.			
3.			
4.			
5.			
6.			
ETC.			

NOTE: When formulating alternatives, be specific. For example, on a list of ways to save money, instead of "Don't buy brand names," you might write "Buy Korvette's toothpaste instead of Crest; it's one-third cheaper and just as effective." This is a much more forceful suggestion than the previous one.

Then choose the three alternatives you like the best and rank order these.

If you would consider using any of the new alternatives in your life, write a Self-Contract (Strategy Number 59, page 254) at this point.

▸ SUGGESTIONS LIST

1. Ways to personally stop polluting our environment.
2. Ways to make new friends.

3. Ways to make learning fun.
4. Ways to get along better with our children (parents, spouse, boss, and so on.)
5. Ways to get the most for our dollar.
6. Ways to make a contribution to our community/school.
7. Ways to make religion more meaningful.
8. What to do when you find yourself taking an unpopular stand on an issue.
9. Ways to make our voices heard in politics.
10. Ways of gaining more control over our own lives.
11. Ways of working more effectively in small groups.
12. Ways to settle family arguments.
13. Ways to handle the overly aggressive male/female on a date.
14. Ways to beautify our community/school.
15. How to give a great party.
16. Exciting things to do with our leisure time.
17. Ways to work for peace.
18. Ways to give someone negative feedback.
19. Ways to criticize a friend about something personal.
20. Things to do and places to go on a date without spending a cent.
21. Ways to save time.
22. Things to do on a weekend in this town.
23. Ways to celebrate spring (autumn, winter, summer).
24. Creative ways to give presents.
25. Ways to earn (save) money.
26. Where to go on a date/vacation.
27. Things to do to improve race relations in our community/school.
28. Ways to eat more healthfully.
29. Ways to get more or better exercise.
30. Ways to express appreciation to a family member.

Alternative Action Search

▸ PURPOSE

Frequently, we find ourselves acting one way in a situation and later regretting it or wishing we had behaved differently. The clearer we are about our values, the more congruent our actions are with our feelings and beliefs and therefore the less often we later regret our actions.

This strategy enables you to consider alternatives for action in various specific situations. The goal is to encourage you to bring your everyday actions more consistently into harmony with your feelings and beliefs.

▸ PROCEDURE

Below are a number of specific situations or vignettes that call for some proposed action. Choose one that interests you. Then, given all your beliefs, feelings, and values related to this vignette, ideally what would you want to do in this situation? Write it out. Then—share it with someone—a friend, family member, or associate. Have them read the situation and ask them what they would do. Compare your responses to the same situation.

► **VIGNETTES**

1. You are walking behind someone. You see her take out a cigarette pack, withdraw the last cigarette, put the cigarette in her mouth, crumple the package, and nonchalantly toss it over her shoulder onto the sidewalk. You are twenty-five feet behind her. Ideally, what would you do?

2. There is a person at work or in your class who has a body odor problem. You know the general sentiment is, "He's not such a bad guy, but I just hate to get near him." You hardly know him—you have sort of a nodding acquaintance at a friendly distance. Ideally, what would you do?

3. You are pushing a shopping cart in a supermarket and you hear a thunderous crash of cans. As you round the corner you see a two-year-old being beaten quite severely by his mother, apparently for pulling out the bottom can of the pyramid. Ideally, what would you do?

4. You are on a vacation trip driving to the beach with your family. You would like to go to the amusement park, but you are concerned because you have spent most of the money you had saved for your vacation earlier. You stop for gasoline, get out, and walk around. A lady is walking back to her car and you see her purse fall open and her wallet fall out. You walk over and pick up the wallet just as the lady gets into her car to drive away. The edges of several $20 bills are sticking out of the wallet. No one saw you pick it up. What would you do?

5. You have forgotten your last two dentist's appointments. The dentist was furious that last time. You

have an appointment today. You look up and see it is exactly 2 P.M., which is when you're supposed to be there. It is a twenty-minute walk to his office and there are no buses. What would you do?

6. You see a kid shoplifting at the local discount store. You're concerned that he'll get into serious trouble if the store detective catches him. What would you do?

7. You're driving on a two-lane road behind another car. You notice that one of the wheels is wobbling more and more. It looks as if the nuts are coming off, one by one. There's no way to pass, because cars are coming in the other direction in a steady stream. What would you do?

8. At a picnic, there is a giant punch bowl. One of the little kids, much to everyone's horror, accidentally drops a whole plate of spaghetti into the punch. What would you do?

9. You're at a party. The hostess is serving the dessert. You know that she is very fussy about cleanliness, but you see that the piece of cream pie she has given your spouse/parent is infested with ants. But only her piece seems to be like that. What would you do?

10. You're taking a really lousy course at the university. You're not doing well in the course. On the week of the final exam, someone offers to sell you a copy of what he claims is the final for only $20. What would you do?

11. You've raised your son/daughter not to play with guns. Your rich uncle comes for a long-awaited visit and, of course, he brings your son/daughter a .22 rifle with lots of ammunition. What would you do?

12. Your spouse (parent) has been giving you a lot of flack about how much TV you watch. One day you come

home from work (school) and the TV set isn't working. You suspect your spouse (parent) has done something to the set. What would you do?

13. Your family is having a discussion about abortion and you notice that your twelve-year-old daughter/son becomes extremely upset. What would you do?

14. You are new in town and you take your car to what is supposed to be the best garage in town. You tell the mechanic you need points and plugs, and you ask routinely for the old plugs and points to be saved so you can see them. The mechanic says, "What's the matter, don't you trust me?" What would you do?

15. At a dinner party you attend, two guests begin to match each other with stereotypical ethnic jokes. What would you do?

16. You're late. You're supposed to have the car back by twelve noon, or it will be real trouble for you. Two blocks away from your house, you hit a dog that runs across the street. What would you do?

17. Your mother tells you that the doctor has just told her that your dad has cancer and has only two months to live. She has decided not to tell him. What would you do?

18. You overhear two coworkers or classmates talking about how they and some others are going to stand outside a gay bar next Saturday night and "bash" some of the customers when they leave the bar. What would you do?

Brainstorming

► PURPOSE

Brainstorming is a well-known, widely used problem-solving tool. It encourages people to use their imaginations and be creative. It helps elicit numerous solutions to any given problem, e.g., "What shall we name this product?" "What should I do in this situation?" "How can we overcome this obstacle?" In the area of values, it is very helpful in eliciting alternatives.

► RULES FOR BRAINSTORMING*

1. No evaluation of any kind is allowed in a thinking-up session. If you judge and evaluate ideas as they come up, it tends to close down spontaneous thinking.
2. Think up as many wild ideas as possible. It is easier to tame down a wild idea than to pep up a bland idea. In fact, if wild ideas are not forthcoming in a brainstorming session, it is usually evidence that you are censoring your ideas.

---

*From an in-service training resource notebook for teachers of the gifted, compiled by William M. Rogge.

3. Quantity is encouraged. Quantity eventually breeds quality. When a great number of ideas come pouring out in rapid succession, evaluation is crowded out. You are free to give your imagination wide range and good ideas result.

4. Build upon or modify your ideas. Combining or modifying previous ideas often leads to new ideas that are superior to those that sparked them.

Brainstorming can be used as an activity in and of itself, or it can be used in conjunction with some of the other values strategies in this book. Here are some brainstorming topics—both serious and silly—that you might work on.

1. How many ways can you think of to make this place a happier, more enjoyable place to be?

2. Your three-ton moving van, loaded with one million pipe cleaners (or balloons, chestnuts, or brassieres) skids off the road and gets stuck in the mud. How many ways can you think up for using your cargo to get your truck out of the mud?

3. What interesting new vacations might you take next year?

4. Here is an object (a mirror, a ruler, a wastepaper basket, or the like). Identify as many ways and purposes as you can for using this object.

5. If your company/school were to change its name, what should the new name be?

NOTE: The suggestions made for Alternatives Search (Strategy Number 23, page 150) and for Alternative Action Search (Strategy Number 24, page 153) can also be used

as brainstorming activities. You can do the brainstorming
activity yourself or, better yet, with your family or a group.
For example:

1. What are all the ways you can think of to redecorate
   your house?
2. What different kinds of office parties or events could
   you have this year?

Consequences Search

► **PURPOSE**

The evaluation of consequences is just as important as the search for alternatives; for if we choose an alternative without thinking about the consequences, we increase the risk of making a poor choice. This strategy gives you practice in searching for the consequences of various alternatives.

► **PROCEDURE**

The Consequences Search strategy can be used by itself, or as a follow-up activity to the Alternatives Search (Strategy Number 23, page 150) or the Alternative Action Search (Strategy Number 24, page 153). For either, construct a Consequences Grid as illustrated.

At the top of the grid you are to place, in the appropriate spaces, the three most feasible solutions you have developed for an action you want to take, for a decision you want to make, or for one of the vignettes presented in the Alternative Action Search, or the three best ideas

CONSEQUENCES GRID

ALTERNATIVE #1:	ALTERNATIVE #2:	ALTERNATIVE #3:

from the Alternatives Search. Then, for each of these three alternatives, you are to list as many possible consequences as you can think of. You can use Brainstorming (Strategy Number 25, page 157) for generating consequences.

Having considered three consequences, you are then to rank the alternatives or decide to drop one or more of the alternatives and look for others. If the latter happens, the activity can be repeated, listing consequences for the newly found alternatives.

NOTE: Sometimes you can think of only one alternative in a particular situation or for a particular problem. In such a case, list that alternative at the top of the first column and put "Not doing alternative number 1" at the top of the second column. (Not to choose is also to make a choice; thus, there are always at least two alternatives.) Then explore the consequences of following the first alternative and the consequences of maintaining the status quo.

Removing Barriers to Action

► **PURPOSE**

Often, we find that of the seven subprocesses of valuing, the ones that are least likely to have been fulfilled are those dealing with acting on our beliefs. We may be willing to take a stand, to prize it and be willing to publicly affirm it, to have chosen it from alternatives freely with knowledge of the consequences, but we may be unwilling or unable to *act* upon it because of perceived or real barriers to action. This strategy is designed to help you identify and remove barriers to action that often block and plague your values development.

► **PROCEDURE**

Write at the top of a paper some action you would like to take or decision you would like to make. It should be an action you are having some difficulty taking or that you fear to take. Then draw a line lengthwise down the middle of the paper. On the right-hand side of the paper, list all the perceived or real barriers, both within and outside yourself, that seem to be keeping you from acting. On the left-hand side of the paper, list steps you could take that might help remove or reduce each of the barriers. Finally, on the back of the paper, develop a plan of action for actually removing the barriers.

In a family or group setting, family or group members can help one another think of ways to remove their barriers to action.

Getting Started

▸ **PURPOSE**

Many of us have grandiose plans we often think or talk about. However, putting these plans into action sometimes seems like a tremendous task. Like the previous strategy (Removing Barriers to Action, Strategy Number 27, page 162), this exercise helps you move toward the action level of valuing. It teaches the habit of looking realistically at what concrete actions are required to begin working toward a goal. It also encourages you to start asking yourself the question, "Am I really doing what I want to do with my life?"

▸ **PROCEDURE**

On a sheet of paper, prepare a chart with three columns, as shown below. Then list up to ten or more things you would like to learn to do or do better. Or use the items we have provided by writing in anything you would like to learn to do or do better in the designated areas.

WHAT I'D LIKE TO LEARN TO DO OR BE ABLE TO DO BETTER	DATE	FIRST STEPS
1. In music:		
2. In art:		
3. In sports:		
4. In relating to people:		
5. In school politics:		
6. In studying:		
7. Socially:		
8. With my family:		
9. Open category:		

Then, from the items you have listed, choose any three that you really would like to get started on. Assign logical, realistic dates to these items. Finally, proceed to list the first steps you will have to take in getting started.

When you finish, ask a friend or family member whether he or she has any other suggestions for first steps and list any of these you care to.

Another variation of this strategy is Ready for Summer (Strategy Number 71, page 291).

Pattern Search

▶ **PURPOSE**

One of the processes of valuing is building a pattern of consistent action. However, many of the things we do that involve patterns are done out of compulsion or habit rather than out of conscious choice. This strategy is designed to help you become aware of the patterns you presently have and of your motives and reasons for doing things in a certain pattern. After completing the Pattern Search strategy, you may continue in your old patterns or you may develop alternative patterns; the important thing is that, whatever you do, you do it on a conscious, free-choice basis.

▶ **PROCEDURE**

On a sheet of paper construct a Patterns Grid, as shown.

PATTERNS GRID

WHAT PROCEDURES DO YOU FOLLOW ABOUT THIS ACTIVITY?	IS IT A PATTERN?		IS IT DONE OUT OF			DO YOU PRIZE YOUR ANSWERS?		
	YES	NO	COM-PULSION	HABIT	FREE CHOICE	YES	NO	?
1.								
2.								
3.								
4.								
5.								
6.								
Etc.								

There are many activities for which people generally follow their own specific patterns. Look over the list we have provided and select several of the items that interest you, or create your own.

List these items on your Patterns Grid and fill in and check the appropriate boxes on the grid.

NOTE: Compulsion here means *outward* compulsion, e.g., "I don't want to get up every morning at 7:00 A.M., but I have to." Habit means an unconscious pattern or inner compulsion, e.g., "I've never really thought about it. I just have always combed my hair in bangs." Free choice means conscious choice, e.g., "I like to make presents for my friends and buy them for my parents." We realize these definitions raise philosophical arguments about free choice. The emphasis in this strategy is on the feeling you have about your pattern. Does the sense of compulsion, the sense of habit, or the sense of free choice feel strongest to you?

The Pattern Search activity may be followed by choosing a pattern you are not particularly happy with and doing an Alternatives Search (Strategy Number 23, page 150) to see if you can come up with ideas for a more fulfilling pattern.

▶ **PATTERN SEARCH QUESTIONS**

What is your pattern for:

1. Parking at a shopping center?
2. Using an escalator or stairs?
3. Revealing your age?
4. Eating at a restaurant? (e.g., Are you concerned with the price or do you order what you want?)
5. Getting places on time?
6. Paying bills?
7. Making friends?
8. Ritual at the dinner table? At Thanksgiving dinner table?
9. How you brush your teeth?
10. Working for grades in a course you take in school?
11. Buying clothes?
12. Making dates?
13. Attending meetings?
14. Responding to seeing gay couples?
15. What you do at a dull meeting?
16. What you dream about at night?
17. What you daydream about?
18. Taking showers or baths?

19. What time you go to bed at night and get up in the morning?

20. How you talk about other people when they are not there?

21. Counting or not counting calories?

22. Answering your phone?

23. Doing your Christmas or holiday shopping?

24. Reading the newspaper?

25. Dealing with your old clothes?

26. Doing protective maintenance on a car, a motorcycle, or a bicycle?

27. Bringing a gift when you are invited to someone's home for dinner?

28. What you serve company for dinner?

29. Handling premium stamps that you get at the grocery store?

30. Parking at a drive-in movie?

31. Praying or meditating?

32. Responding when you witness someone littering?

33. Watching movies on TV?

34. Reading your mail?

35. Crying in movies?

36. Getting out of going to parties you don't really want to go to?

37. Disposing of your dirty clothes at the end of the day?

38. Buying the large, economy size of things?

39. Making long-distance phone calls?

40. Writing letters?

41. Exercising?

42. What you wear?

43. How you wear or comb your hair?

44. Doing your bookwork/homework?

45. Speaking up in groups?

46. Giving presents?
47. Sexual behavior on dates?
48. Voting in elections?
49. Cooking at home?
50. Contributing to charities or causes?

Three Characters

▸ PURPOSE

This strategy helps you become clearer about your own goals and purposes in life. By identifying with other peoples' achievements and characteristics, you can help yourself forge your own values.

▸ PROCEDURE

If you could not be yourself but someone else, what is the name of the character you would most like to be? Write down on a piece of paper the name of the person chosen from real life, fiction, the news, movies, literature, cartoons, history, or the like.

Then write down the name of a character you would least like to be like.

Then write down the name of a character who is most like you.

When you have listed your three characters, write down the reasons for making your selections. Then ask yourself values-clarifying questions like: "Were my characters males or females? Can I think of anyone whose list of characters I would be on? Would my list have been different three years ago? Would my best friend be able to guess the names on my list? Who would be or have been on my parents' lists?"

Chairs or Dialogue with Self*

► PURPOSE

When we are confronted with a values conflict, choice, or dilemma, several voices within our heads begin operating. One voice says, "Do this"; another voice says, "No, do that." Often a third or more voices offer new alternatives and new perspectives.

This strategy teaches you a useful method for clarifying the issue at stake in a values conflict. It is a helpful tool in the decision-making process. It also graphically demonstrates that values decisions are rarely easy ones, and helps you to accept and work with some of the confusion you might experience within yourself.

► PROCEDURE

Tune in on your internal voices by choosing a conflict you have been having in which your internal voices have been carrying on a dialogue. The dialogue might be about whether to save your earnings to buy a new car or to go on

*This strategy is an adaptation of a common technique in Gestalt therapy.

an expensive vacation. Or it might be a decision about whether or not to tell a loved one or friend something important. Then write a short dialogue or script of the conversation between your internal voices.

When you have finished writing your dialogue, place two chairs facing each other. Sit in one chair and start the dialogue you have written, then move to the second chair to answer yourself. Continue in this manner, switching chairs to talk to and answer yourself, until you have completed your script. Then go on acting out your internal voices as long as you can or until you reach a resolution of the conflict.

NOTE: Focus on the conscious choices you are confronting and the conscious pro and con feelings and reasons you express.

If you do this activity in a family or group setting, act out your dialogue in front of the others. Then, when you have taken it as far as you can or want to go, you can ask another family or group member to take one of the chairs and, from that position, continue to engage you in dialogue. This can produce new and valuable perspectives on your dilemma.

Percentage Questions

▶ PURPOSE

The Either/or Forced Choice (Strategy Number 5, page 69) provides us with a relatively simple index of our feelings on various pairs of alternatives. However, in many cases, life is not an either/or situation, but one involving more complex decisions. This strategy introduces the concept of percentage thinking and provides you with an opportunity to examine your priorities.

▶ PROCEDURE

Look over the list of percentage questions we have provided. Select those that interest or apply to you. Write down your answers next to each question.

The activity may be followed by I Learned Statements (Strategy Number 15, page 126).

▶ PERCENTAGE QUESTIONS

What percentage of:

1. your salary would you like to give to charity?
2. your salary would you like to give to the church or religious institution?

3. the first class letters you receive do you answer?

4. your salary (or allowance) do you spend on gifts?

5. the defects in your home would you reveal to a prospective buyer?

6. women should we have in the U.S. Congress?

7. the labor force should be unemployed before the government should take some action?

8. your income should be set aside in case of an emergency?

9. your time at home should be devoted to keeping the house clean?

10. your time would you like to spend with your family?

11. minorities would you like to have living in your neighborhood? of whites?

12. your time do you spend working for a cause you really believe in?

13. government elections do you vote in?

14. time do you spend sleeping?

15. time do you spend working?

16. your coworkers/classmates would you call friends?

17. parents/teachers do you think really love kids?

18. your time is spent doing things you really don't want to do each day?

19. your life could you describe as being very happy?

20. your free time do you spend reading books?

21. your free time do you spend watching TV?

22. the time do you spend listening to music, without doing anything else, just listening?

23. tax monies should go toward defense spending? AIDS research? cancer research? crime prevention?

24. the people you send Christmas or holiday cards to do you hope you will get one from?

25. your weekend should be devoted to maintenance of your house or apartment?

26. your total reading time would you like to spend on pure nonsense? on mysteries? on newspapers? on magazines?

27. your day would you like time to do absolutely nothing?

28. the time that you drive do you drive above the speed limit?

29. the times that someone asks you if you like what they are wearing do you tell the absolute truth?

30. of an elementary schoolchild's free time do you think should be allotted to TV watching?

31. of your earnings or allowance would you like to save for future use? What percentage *do* you save?

32. of your dates would you like to be double dates?

33. of your free time do you spend alone, with relatives, with friends?

34. of your money do you spend on clothes, food, movies and other amusements, books or magazines, other things?

35. of your courses in school do you enjoy?

36. are you a Volkswagen and what percentage a Cadillac? What percentage a forest and what percentage a meadow? [In other words, all the Either/or Forced Choices (Strategy Number 5, page 69) can easily be changed to Percentage Questions.]

The Pie of Life

▶ PURPOSE

This strategy is a variation of Percentage Questions (Strategy Number 32, page 175). In its simplest form, it asks us to inventory our lives—to see how we actually *do* spend our time, our money, and so on. The Pie of Life can raise some thought-provoking questions about how we live our lives. This information is needed if we hope to move from what we are getting to what we want to get out of life.

▶ PROCEDURE

Draw a large circle on a sheet of paper to represent a segment of your life. Now look at how you use a typical day. Divide your circle into four quarters using dotted lines. Each slice represents six hours. Estimate how many hours or parts of an hour you spend on each of the following areas on a typical day. How many hours do you spend:

1. On SLEEP?
2. At WORK, at a job that earns you money?

3. In SCHOOL?
4. COMMUTING to work or school?
5. With FRIENDS, socializing, playing sports, and so on?
6. On BOOKWORK/HOMEWORK?
7. ALONE, playing, reading, watching TV?
8. On CHORES around the house?
9. With FAMILY, including mealtimes?
10. On MISCELLANEOUS other pastimes?

Your estimates will not be exact, but they should add up to twenty-four, the number of hours in everyone's day. Draw slices in your pie to represent proportionately the part of the day you spend on each category. Your pie may look something like this:

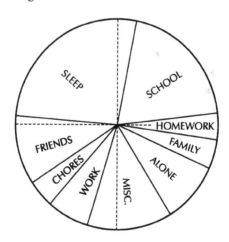

Now reflect on these questions and write about them in your values journal (Strategy Number 17, page 130).

1. Are you satisfied with the relative sizes of your slices?
2. Ideally, how big would you want each slice to be? Draw your ideal pie.

3. Realistically, is there anything you can do to begin to change the size of some of your slices?
4. Is there a Self-Contract (Strategy Number 59, page 254) you'd be willing to make and sign your name to?

If time permits, take any one segment (for example, FAMILY) and make another pie to break down the time spent in that category. For example, if the whole family pie represents five or six hours, each dotted segment is an hour and a quarter or an hour and a half. Plot a typical family "day," putting in the time for meals, play, working together, praying, socializing, watching TV, and so on—whatever you do as a family. You might do one pie for a typical weekday and another one for a typical Sunday.

After each pie is executed, the above series of values journal questions are again addressed.

NOTE: There is no right way to divide up a pie. Each of us lives a different life. There is no implication that it is necessary to change the time devoted to any specific category. The focus is on inventorying and looking at your life more closely. Any decisions to change are up to you.

There are many things that can be looked at in terms of slices of the pie of life, for example, a pie on where the money goes each week, on the kinds of clothes hanging in your closet, on the music you listen to, the books, magazines, and newspapers you read, the people who visit your home, the types of charities and causes you contribute time or money to, or the like.

In addition to being a factual inventory of your lives, The Pie of Life can ask for a subjective inventory. For example, you can plot the proportions of the day that you feel HIGH, NEUTRAL, or LOW. Or a WORK pie can be drawn to show the portions that are CREATIVE, INTER-ESTING, DULL but important, and BUSYWORK (dull and relatively unimportant).

Whenever you examine how you divide a pie of life now, as you are actually living it, the inevitable and important follow-up questions can be asked: "How would I ideally like to divide this pie?"

In a family or group setting if people are willing, it is interesting to share your pies of life, to see how the different family or group members were similar or different in how you drew your pies.

Magic Box*

▶ **PURPOSE**

To help you think about what you value.

▶ **PROCEDURE**

Imagine that you have been given a magic box that is very special. It is capable of making itself very small or very large. Best of all, it can contain anything you want it to contain. It can have anything you want, tangible or intangible. Write down your answer.

You might then ask other questions like:

1. What would you want in a magic box for your family?
2. What would you want for your best friend?
3. What is the smallest thing you would want?
4. What is the largest thing?
5. What would you want for poor people?

Keep what you write in your Values Journal (Strategy Number 17, page 130). After you have done this activity

---

*Thanks to Jack Canfield for this idea.

several times, Rank Order (Strategy Number 4, page 42) the things you want most for yourself. Then ask yourself if you have been doing anything to attain these things.

All About Me

▶ **PURPOSE**

This strategy provides you with an opportunity to think and make statements about your life in a systematic, ongoing way. It could be considered another version of The Values Journal or the Values Data Bank (Strategy Number 17, page 130) and is also similar to Pages for an Autobiography (Strategy Number 36, page 186).

▶ **PROCEDURE**

Each day for a week, write a story or essay in your values journal. Stories are to be titled:

Day 1: Who Am I?
Day 2: Who Takes Care of Me?
Day 3: I Am Proud . . .
Day 4: Someday I Want to Be . . .
Day 5: My Funniest Experience
Day 6: If I Could Change the World
Day 7: My Friend

Unfinished Sentences (Strategy Number 37, page 190) provide many ideas for stories.

In a family or group setting, have each person do this activity for a week, writing on the same topics. You can choose story topics that are of particular relevance to your family or group. Then, when the week is over, come together and give each person the chance to read aloud any one of his or her essays. If you prefer, each person could read his or her story on the *same* topic.

Pages for an Autobiography

► **PURPOSE**

This strategy helps you develop an awareness of your life patterns through specific recall of both important and seemingly inconsequential events in your past.

► **PROCEDURE**

Assume you have decided to write your autobiography. An easy way to do this is to develop pages for your autobiography by recalling certain events from your past. (See specific suggestions below.) Then you are to examine these experiences to see if you can detect important life patterns. Finally, you are to judge which of these life patterns have been formed out of conscious choice and which are the result of outside pressures or inner compulsions.

► **SUGGESTED PAGES FOR YOUR AUTOBIOGRAPHY**

1. Draw a line across the top of your paper. Mark one end Birth and the other end with your present age. Place an X along the line for each time you changed

your hairstyle and write the approximate age underneath each X. Now write a story about why you changed your hairstyle each time, what it looked like before and after, what you thought of it at the time, and how you feel about making that change now.

2. What have you done on the New Year's Eves of your life? In one or two sentences, briefly describe as many New Year's Eves as you can remember, in chronological order. What does this chronology say to you about yourself—now and in the past—and what does it show about your developing values?

3. Who have your important teachers been—not only in school, but all those people, young or old, in school or out, who taught you what you regarded, then or now, as valuable lessons in your life?

4. Draw a line across the page and mark one end Birth and the other end your present age. Place an X along the line for each turning point in your life and place your approximate age underneath each X. Now write a story describing the turning points, how they occurred, how you felt at the time, and how you feel about them now.

5. Make a list of the best friends you have had throughout your life. Write a little about how you met, what you did together, why you liked each other, why you may have drifted apart. Who is or are your best friends now? Is your present pattern with your friends similar or different from your pattern in the past?

► **ADDITIONAL SUGGESTIONS**

6. How did you learn to ride a bicycle? Who helped?*
7. Who taught you how to dance? Where?

*Thanks to Richard Davis for several of these Pages for an Autobiography.

8. When did you first learn how to jump rope?

9. Who taught you Monopoly, poker, or chess?

10. How did you first learn to kiss? Make love?

11. How many different places have you lived in your life? Tell when, where, and why you moved.

12. What modes of transportation have you used during your life?

13. How did you celebrate your last five birthdays?

14. With what organizations have you been affiliated?

15. What kinds of furniture have you lived with?

16. What did you do with your summers? List as many as you can remember.

17. What collections have you made during your life?

18. What songs have been your favorites during your life?

19. Recall any serious accidents or illnesses you have had.

20. List all the churches or temples you have attended services in.

21. Recall all the birthday presents you have given your mother or father in the last five to ten years.

22. Recall all the ceremonies you have taken part in.

23. Recall the last five times you have cried. What was each about?

24. Recall all the animals you have ever had for pets.

25. Recall all the trips you have taken in the last ten years.

26. What have been the highlights of this past year? The low points?

27. Think of all the things you have wanted to be (job occupations) since you can remember.

28. What in your life made you feel the happiest? The saddest?

29. List your greatest successes in life. Your greatest failures.
30. List all the times you have thought life was hopeless and hardly worth living.
31. Mention some of the books that have touched your life deeply.
32. What were some of the phonograph records that have meant a lot to you?
33. List all the people you've been in love with.
34. Recall certain tests or examinations that are still vivid memories.
35. Describe any or all of the close brushes with death you have had.
36. Recall several items of clothing that were your favorites at one time or another.
37. Who taught you how to drive a car?
38. How did you learn to type?
39. Where did you learn manners?
40. Think of something else you know how to do, and record where you learned it and from whom.

Unfinished Sentences

▸ **PURPOSE**

This strategy helps you reveal and explore some of your attitudes, beliefs, actions, convictions, interests, aspirations, likes, dislikes, goals, and purposes—in other words, your values indicators. What often emerges from this activity is a growing awareness of your developing values.

▸ **PROCEDURE**

Look over the list of unfinished sentences below. Select a number of those that interest or apply to you. Complete them in writing.

Then code your completed sentences with the following codes:

a. Place a P in front of those items of which you are *proud.*
b. Place a PA in front of those items you would be willing to *publicly affirm.*
c. Place a CA in front of those items for which you *considered alternatives.*

d. Place a TC in front of those items you have *thoughtfully considered*, perhaps even anticipating the consequences.

e. Place a CF in front of those items where you feel you were able to *choose freely*.

f. Place an A in front of those items you have *acted upon*.

g. Place a PB in front of those items that are or indicate *patterns of behavior* in your life.

File your sentences away for the present. At a later date, when you have completed several lists, take out all of your completed sentences and look for patterns.

NOTE: In a family or group setting, the leader whips around the room calling on people to complete aloud any one of the sentences with whatever comes to mind. There can be a second or third time around if there is time and the group seems interested. Of course, anyone may pass. A discussion can follow, with people elaborating on their answers or questioning other members about their answers.

▸ UNFINISHED SENTENCE STEMS

1. I wish the president would . . .
2. On vacations, I like to . . .
3. I'd like to tell my best friend . . .
4. Our community would be better if . . .
5. If I had an extra $500, I would . . .
6. Many people don't agree with me about . . .
7. The happiest day in my life was . . .
8. Some people seem to want only to . . .
9. I believe . . .

10. If I were five years older . . .
11. My advice to the governor would be . . .
12. If I had a gun I would . . .
13. My favorite vacation place would be . . .
14. When I'm alone at home, I . . .
15. My bluest days are . . .
16. My best friend can be counted on to . . .
17. I am best at . . .
18. Something unique about me is . . .
19. People can hurt my feelings most by . . .
20. Men who wear an earring in the ear are . . .
21. Those with whom I work the closest are . . .
22. In a group I am . . .
23. If someone asked me to organize a new group . . .
24. When other people are upset and hurt in a meeting, I . . .
25. With my boss (teacher) . . .
26. The kind of person who always asks the boss (teacher) for directions . . .
27. People who seldom let me know where they stand . . .
28. People who agree with me make me feel . . .
29. Strong independent people . . .
30. When people depend upon me, I . . .
31. I get angry when . . .
32. I have accomplished . . .
33. Being part of a group that has been together for a long time . . .
34. I get real pleasure from being part of a group when . . .
35. People who expect a lot from me make me feel . . .
36. Other people are frightened most by . . .
37. The things that amuse me most are . . .
38. I feel warmest toward a person when . . .
39. I like best the kind of person who . . .

40. At work/in school I do best when . . .
41. If I feel I can't get across to another person . . .
42. What I want most in life is . . .
43. When someone hurts me, I . . .
44. I often find myself . . .
45. I have difficulty trying to deal with . . .
46. When I see an associate (a classmate) always agreeing with the boss (teacher) . . .
47. When there are heated arguments in a meeting, I . . .
48. I am . . .
49. People who know me well think I am . . .
50. My boss (teacher) thinks I am . . .
51. People who work for (with) me think I am . . .
52. I used to be . . .
53. What I want most out of my job (school) . . .
54. If I had it to do all over again, I would . . .
55. My greatest strength is . . .
56. I need to improve most in . . .
57. I am concerned most about . . .
58. It makes me most uncomfortable when . . .
59. I would consider it risky . . .
60. The subject I would be most reluctant to discuss here is . . .
61. When I enter a new group, I feel . . .
62. When people first meet me, they . . .
63. When someone does all the talking, I . . .
64. I feel most productive when a leader . . .
65. In a group, I am most afraid of . . .
66. I am happiest when . . .
67. I feel loneliest in a group when . . .
68. I trust those who . . .
69. I feel closest to someone when . . .
70. I feel loved most when . . .

71. An overweight/underweight person . . .
72. On Saturdays, I like to . . .
73. If I had five days to live . . .
74. If I had my own car . . .
75. I feel best when people . . .
76. If I had a million dollars I would . . .
77. Secretly I wish . . .
78. My children won't have to . . .
79. God is . . .

UNFINISHED SENTENCES FOR YOUNGER CHILDREN

1. If I had another week of summer vacation I would . . .
2. I am most creative when . . .
3. If I had $1, I would . . .
4. An important learning experience was . . .
5. The thing that scares me most is . . .
6. Someday I am going to . . .
7. Some people always seem to want . . .
8. People I like always . . .
9. The people in my neighborhood are . . .
10. I cry when . . .
11. I'm afraid to . . .
12. Something I'm really interested in is . . .
13. I'm happy when . . .
14. When I grow up, I want to be . . .
15. The funniest thing I ever saw was . . .
16. I feel most confident when . . .
17. The trouble with being honest (dishonest) is . . .
18. I like people who . . .
19. If I could introduce a bill into Congress, I would . . .
20. Twenty years from now, I hope this country . . .
21. I feel happiest of all when . . .

22. If I saw someone shoplifting in a store, I would . . .
23. Motorcycles make me . . .
24. I'm trying to overcome my fear . . .
25. To say what I really, really believe . . .
26. When my family gets together . . .
27. If I become a father or a mother, I . . .

Who Comes to Your House?

▶ **PURPOSE**

Value indicators are often found in our choice of friend-ships and associations. This strategy is designed to help you become more aware of your friendship patterns and values related to friendship.

▶ **PROCEDURE**

On a sheet of paper draw a line down the middle. On the left-hand side of the paper, list the initials of all the people you have invited to your house for a meal in the last year. (Younger children can list those they have had over to play.) On the right side of the paper, list the initials of all the people who have invited you to their houses for a meal in the past year.

Then code both columns, placing the following letters or symbols next to each name or initial:

1. R if the person was a relative, F for a friend, O for other.

2. M if the person's manners bother you.

3. P if the person generally brings a present.

4. Star the names of those people whom you are really happy to see when they come over, and on the other side, those people who you think are really happy to see you when you come over.

5. X if it wouldn't matter much if the person didn't come back or if the person didn't invite you back again.

6. S or D to indicate whether their religion is the same or different from yours.

7. SR or DR to indicate whether the person is the same race or a different race from yours.

I Learned Statements (Strategy Number 15, page 126) or I Wonder Statements (Strategy Number 16, page 128) are good follow-ups to this activity.

To use in a family or group setting, have each person share his or her I Learned or I Wonder Statements with the family or group members.

Strength of Values*

▶ **PURPOSE**

This strategy provides you with an opportunity to assess the strength of your feelings on values issues that you identify.

▶ **PROCEDURE**

On the following worksheet, complete the unfinished sentences or make them into paragraphs if you wish. The worksheet may then be filed for later reference.

In a family or group setting, after individuals complete the worksheet, go around the group and give each member a chance to read one of his or her completed sentences or paragraphs. Each person can also discuss what they learned or relearned about him/herself from doing the worksheet.

▶ **WORKSHEET**

Complete the following statements. You may write one sentence or a whole paragraph. Write *nothing* for any

*Thanks to Hanoch McCarty for this activity.

sentence for which you have no answer or *pass* if you'd prefer not to say.

1. I would be willing to die for . . .
2. I would be willing to physically fight for . . .
3. I would argue strongly in favor of . . .
4. I would quietly take a position in favor of . . .
5. I will share only with my friends my belief that . . .
6. I prefer to keep to myself my belief that . . .

Strongly Agree/Strongly Disagree*

► **PURPOSE**

This strategy allows you to examine the strength of your feelings about a given series of values issues. It serves many of the same purposes as the Values Continuum (Strategy Number 8, page 87) except that you are not allowed to take a middle or neutral stand.

► **PROCEDURE**

Complete the following worksheet, which contains a series of belief statements.

Interpret the belief statements as you wish. There is no single correct way to interpret them. They are to be used simply as thought and discussion starters.

► **WORKSHEET**

Instructions: Circle the response that most closely indicates the way you feel about each item:

---

*Thanks to Dale V. Alam for his developmental work on this strategy. Thanks to Sandy Parisi for examples 17 to 35.

SA = Strongly Agree
AS = Agree Somewhat
DS = Disagree Somewhat
SD = Strongly Disagree

Response   *Item*

SA AS DS SD   **1.** People are losing respect for each other.

SA AS DS SD   **2.** People are basically good.

SA AS DS SD   **3.** Giving grades encourages meaningful learning in school.

SA AS DS SD   **4.** There is a life after death.

SA AS DS SD   **5.** I am racially prejudiced.

SA AS DS SD   **6.** I would discourage premarital sex for my son.

SA AS DS SD   **7.** I would encourage premarital sex for my daughter.

SA AS DS SD   **8.** I prefer police brutality to riots.

SA AS DS SD   **9.** Marijuana should be legalized.

SA AS DS SD   **10.** Familiarity breeds contempt.

SA AS DS SD   **11.** Government has become too big and powerful.

SA AS DS SD   **12.** Religion or spirituality play an important part in my life.

SA AS DS SD   **13.** Homosexual couples should be allowed to legally marry.

SA AS DS SD   **14.** People convicted of three felonies should go to jail for life.

SA AS DS SD   **15.** We have enough environmental protection laws.

SA AS DS SD   **16.** No individual or group should be allowed to contribute more than $100 to a political campaign.

SA AS DS SD **17.** The constitutional right to assembly should include the right of Ku Klux Klan members to march on Main Street, USA.*

SA AS DS SD **18.** Public funding should be allowed for single-sex universities.

SA AS DS SD **19.** A moment of silence at the beginning of the school day does not violate the First Amendment separation of church and state.

SA AS DS SD **20.** Public funding should be allowed for single-race universities.

SA AS DS SD **21.** A parent in a public school system should not be permitted to remove his/her child from a class taught by a homosexual.

SA AS DS SD **22.** All government publications should be printed in both English and Spanish.

SA AS DS SD **23.** A college professor should be prohibited from dating his or her students.

SA AS DS SD **24.** The right to bear arms should permit every American to own a handgun.

SA AS DS SD **25.** Public funding of abortion should be permitted.

SA AS DS SD **26.** Smokers have no rights.

SA AS DS SD **27.** Barbie is a legitimate role model for young girls.

SA AS DS SD **28.** A parent should not permit his/her child to play with toy guns.

SA AS DS SD **29.** Women should have an equal chance to be in combat roles in the military.

SA AS DS SD **30.** A man should hold a door open for a woman when approaching an entrance.

SA AS DS SD   **31.** Parents should permit their children to address adults by their first name.

SA AS DS SD   **32.** Teachers should permit their students to address them by their first name.

SA AS DS SD   **33.** Student lockers should not be subject to a random search.

SA AS DS SD   **34.** Condoms should be distributed to students in schools.

SA AS DS SD   **35.** A professor in a public university should be able to teach his thesis that the Holocaust never occurred.

NOTE: Additional belief statements may be constructed by turning the interview questions in Strategy Number 12 (page 107) into pro and con statements. Reaction Statements (Strategy Number 76, page 309) can also be converted into Strongly Agree/Strongly Disagree statements.

To use in a family or group setting, we suggest using the Family or Group-Values Focus Game (Strategy Number 18, page 132) to help facilitate the values exploration. The focus person can share his or her Strongly Agree/Disagree responses on the item(s) chosen from above, or on the one(s) selected by the family or group.

Taking a Stand*

► **PURPOSE**

This strategy provides you with an opportunity to take a stand that you believe in on a controversial issue.

► **PROCEDURE**

Select a controversial issue—something that people have strong feelings about. Then write a slogan about that issue on a sheet of construction paper or cardboard. The following are examples of slogans on energy and the environment:

DON'T BE A LITTERBUG!

SAVE A TREE—USE RECYCLED PAPER!

SAVE A TREE—EAT A BEAVER!

GIVE A HOOT—DON'T POLLUTE!

ENVIRONMENTALISTS ARE FOR THE BIRDS!

*Thanks to Dale V. Alam for the original idea for this strategy.

SAVE THE WHALES!

THERE IS NO ENERGY CRISIS!

SAVE THE REDWOODS!

PROGRESS BEFORE POLLIWOGS!

NO MORE NUCLEAR PLANTS!

IF YOU NEED A JOB—EAT AN ENVIRONMENTALIST!

RIDE A BIKE TO WORK!

Then post your statement where others will see it, post it on a button and wear it, write to your congressperson, or send a letter to the editor expressing your stand on the issue and the reasoning behind the stand.

In a family or group setting, have members share their reasons for taking the stand reflected by their slogan.

Values in Action

► **PURPOSE**

This strategy focuses on the action side of valuing. It helps you see alternatives for action and asks you to find some form of action that suits you. Finally, the strategy requires you to actually engage in a planned action to bring about some desired change and then to evaluate the results of your action.

► **PROCEDURE**

Make a list of five changes you think would improve some aspect of your community, state or country, or group. Or select several issues and describe five changes you would like to see made in any of these areas. Then complete the "You Can Do Something About It" worksheet below by putting a check by any of the alternatives you have ever done and an asterisk next to any of the alternatives you would consider doing.

Select one of your five changes and identify which types of action could be used to work toward the change you want to effect. Finally, select two types of action, and for a period of a month, actually engage in both of these actions to bring about the desired change.

A month later, evaluate what you did and what results, if any, occurred.

▶ **WORKSHEET**

You Can Do Something About It!

Most of us, when we see something wrong, want to try to do something about it. Often, however, we remain inactive because we don't know what we might do. Below are some things people have done to achieve desired changes. Which of these acts is your way of doing something?

CAUTION: All action should be informed action; consequently, reading, learning, interviewing, discussing, and generally becoming better informed are necessary first steps before doing something.

WRITE A LETTER

_____ **1.** Write a letter to the editor of your local newspaper. People read these columns more frequently than almost any other section of the daily newspaper. You can influence public opinion.

_____ **2.** Write a letter to your congressperson or senators. Compliment them for something they have done about a problem you are concerned about. Washington counts those letters. They really are influenced by the mail from home.

_____ 3. Send a letter to someone in the news who has done something you respect or admire. You would be surprised how lonely it can be for someone who has made the news for doing something different.

ATTEND A MEETING OR ORGANIZE ONE

_____ 1. Write one of the organizations working for a cause you believe in and ask to be put on the mailing list announcing meetings.

_____ 2. Scan the newspaper for announcements of open meetings of groups in which you are interested.

_____ 3. Ask your own club or civic group, church group, or the like to have a meeting or invite in a guest speaker on a topic you are deeply concerned with. Program chairpersons are always looking for good meeting ideas. They probably will be glad to let you help.

TAKE PART IN SOME ACTION

_____ 1. You can distribute leaflets from door to door, or at a subway entrance.

_____ 2. Picketing may be your cup of tea; it often has an impact.

_____ 3. Organize a petition drive. Even twenty signatures could make news or cause some public official to take notice.

_____ 4. Interview people who are in a position to influence others. Sometimes just a series of perceptive questions can make an issue come alive.

_____ 5. Wear a button or post a slogan or bumper sticker.

_____ **6.** Take part in a peaceful march or in some other demonstration.

_____ **7.** Go as a member of a delegation to see some official on an issue.

FACE-TO-FACE ACTS

_____ **1.** Speak up for your point of view. (For example, if someone expresses a racial or religious stereotype, talk to him about your point of view.)

_____ **2.** Try to get someone to read a pamphlet or an article that argues for a different position than the one he holds.

_____ **3.** Try to close the gap between what you say and what you do. Let your life be a living argument for what you believe in.

Use the rest of this page to list any additional ideas you have about what people can do. YOU CAN DO SOMETHING. Yes, you!

Letters to the Editor

▶ **PURPOSE**

Making a public affirmation is one of the processes in developing values. One of the best (and cheapest) forums for public affirmation is the letters-to-the-editor page of the daily newspaper. It is democracy in action, and Tom Paine would have given his right arm for a chance at such a broad audience. Readership surveys show that the letters-to-the-editor section is one of the most widely and consistently read sections of the typical newspaper.

This strategy, a variation of Values in Action (Strategy Number 42, page 206), asks you to make a public affirmation to the community at large. For many people, breaking into print has been a real affirmation of both the power of the pen and the right of the citizen to shape his or her world.

▶ **PROCEDURE**

Write and mail a letter to the editor of any newspaper or magazine in the country. If your letter gets printed, clip it out and save it in your Values Journal (Strategy Number 17, page 130). Then try another letter to the editor.

You can do this activity in a family or group setting by having the whole family or group collectively draft a letter to the editor, signing the family or group name for publication. Or each member of the family or group could write his or her own letter—on one subject or on different issues.

I Urge Telegrams

► PURPOSE

This strategy provides a simple means by which you can clearly state something that is important to you. Often, the expression of urgency encourages you to then take some action in your own life.

► PROCEDURE

On a 4 × 6–inch card or piece of paper, write out a Western Union telegram message to a real person, beginning with these words: "I urge you to. . . ." The message is to consist of fifteen words or less (or fifty words for a night letter). Sign your name to the telegram.

I Urge Telegrams can be written to nationally known politicians in Washington, to local officials, to people in the entertainment or the sports world, or even to relatives or friends. In each case, the telegram should reflect something you, the sender, feels is important, something you value.

For the next, optional step, call Western Union and actually send the telegram.

Place each telegram in a folder (see the Values Journal or the Values Data Bank, Strategy Number 17, page 130), and when you have written six, spread them out on your desk and make I Learned Statements (Strategy Number 15, page 126) about them and about yourself.

► VARIATION

For each I Urge Telegram you wrote, try rewriting the same telegram as though you are sending it to yourself. You may have to alter the wording somewhat to fit yourself. Often the things we urge others to do say as much about ourselves as they do about the other person. Reversing the telegram is a way to examine how the values issues in the telegram pertain to our own lives.

Diaries

► **PURPOSE**

Perhaps *the* best place to find the data for values-clarification activities is in our own lives. Diaries is a strategy that enables you to collect an enormous amount of information about yourself and examine it.

► **PROCEDURE**

Choose one of the Diaries. (See examples of diary topics below.)

For a whole week, or longer, keep your own individual diary. If you have chosen a Religion Diary, record all thoughts, conversation, and actions having to do with religion. If it is a Budget Diary, accurately record all income and expenditures you made that week. In a Disagreements Diary, record the basic facts about any disagreements you found yourself in that week—whether or not you voiced disagreement at the time. You could also record disagreements between other people that you witnessed.

At the end of the week, review your diary and do I Learned Statements (Strategy Number 15, page 126).

Then ask yourself a series of values-clarifying questions related to your particular dairy.

FOR EXAMPLE, FOR THE DISAGREEMENTS DIARY:

1. On what percentage of the Disagreements did I voice my disagreement?
2. In how many of the disagreements did I find myself actually angry?
3. What is my pattern of handling disagreements?
4. In watching other people's disagreements, did I see any examples of ways of handling conflict that I'd like to employ in my own life?

OR FOR THE BUDGET DIARY:

1. Which expenditures brought me a good deal of pleasure? Which proved disappointing?
2. How many expenditures did I make alone? For how many were other people present? Do I spend more easily when I'm by myself or with others?
3. How many expenditures would I label free choices?
4. Knowing what I know now, what if anything do I wish I had done differently about my income or expenditures?

This activity can be followed with Self-Contracts (Strategy Number 59, page 254).

► SAMPLE DIARIES

1. Time Diary (how the twenty-four hours of each day are spent)

2. Budget Diary
3. Politics Diary
4. Religion Diary
5. Independence Diary
6. Male–Female Roles Diary
7. Disagreements Diary
8. Compliments Diary
9. High Points Diary
10. Affectionate and Tender Feelings Diary
11. Hostility and Anger Diary
12. Low Points Diary
13. Decisions Diary
14. Doubts Diary
15. Any of the areas of confusion and conflict discussed in Part One (pages 4–5) can become the subject of the diary.

Unfinished Business

▸ PURPOSE

Inevitably, as people get personally involved with one another in their search for values, they develop unfinished business—that is, they will have things they would like to talk about further but that were interrupted because of lack of time. This strategy provides you with a convenient tool to settle things you would like to go back and discuss with friends, family, or group members.

▸ PROCEDURE

The idea behind unfinished business is that any time you have a free moment at home/work/school, you might approach someone with whom you have unfinished business and say, "I have some unfinished business with you. Do you have time to talk?"

Unfinished business can take the form of:

a. A question
b. A compliment or some personal praise

c. Constructive criticism or some negative feedback
d. The resumption of a discussion that was interrupted
e. A statement you would like to make to someone
f. Other feelings you would like to share

▸ **EXAMPLES**

"I have some unfinished business with you regarding that argument at the restaurant."

"I have some unfinished business with you. You did something last week in the room that was great, and I didn't tell you . . ."

"I was wondering what you meant this morning when you said . . ."

NOTE: It is important to note that unfinished business can be positive, negative, or neutral—praise, criticism, or just an unresolved issue, unanswered question, or unfinished conversation.

Personal Coat of Arms*

► PURPOSE

Some of the most important questions that will result from values-clarification activities are: "What am I doing with my life? Am I simply settling? Am I just reacting to others or am I in control of the direction of my life? Is my life making a difference?" This activity is an enjoyable way of helping you think about these questions.

► PROCEDURE

On a sheet of paper, draw a coat of arms like the one on the following page. Then answer each of the following questions by drawing, in the appropriate area on your coat of arms, a picture, design, or symbol.

---

*Our thanks to Sr. Louise Romero for this activity.

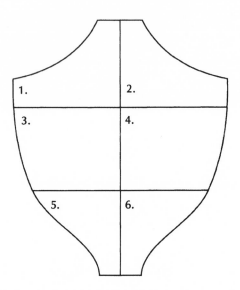

1. What do you regard as your greatest personal achievement to date?
2. What do you regard as your family's greatest achievement?
3. What is the one thing that other people can do to make you happy?
4. What do you regard as your own greatest personal failure to date?
5. What would you do if you had one year to live and were guaranteed success in whatever you attempted?
6. What three things would you most like to be said of you if you died today?

NOTE: Do not use words except in area number 6. Artwork doesn't count. The drawings can be simple, incomplete, and even unintelligible to others, as long as you know what they express.

Other values questions may be substituted, for example:

1. What is something about which you would never budge?
2. What is something you are striving to become? Or to be?
3. What one thing would you want to accomplish by the time you are sixty-five?
4. Draw three things you are good at.
5. What is a personal motto you live by?

Your coat of arms can be shared with other members of your family or group, as you explain the meaning that some or all of your symbols have for you.

You can also do a Family Coat of Arms or Group Coat of Arms to symbolize some of the important achievements, values, and so on of your family or group.

The Fallout-Shelter Problem*

► **PURPOSE**

This is a simulated problem-solving exercise. It raises a host of values issues that you must attempt to work through in a rational manner. It is often a very dramatic example of how our values differ and how we often have trouble listening to people whose beliefs are different from our own.

► **PROCEDURE**

Imagine that you are a member of a department in Washington, D.C., that is in charge of experimental stations in the far outposts of civilization. Suddenly the Third World War breaks out and bombs begin dropping. Places all across the globe are being destroyed. People are heading for whatever fallout shelters are available. You receive a desperate call from one of your experimental stations asking for help.

It seems there are ten people who want shelter but there

*Thanks to Joe Levin for this activity.

is only enough space, air, food, and water in their fallout shelter for six people for a period of three months—which is how long they estimate they can safely stay down there. They realize that if they have to decide among themselves which six should go into the shelter, they are likely to become irrational and begin fighting. So they have decided to call your department and leave the decision to you. They will abide by your decision.

But you quickly have to get ready to head down to your own fallout shelter. So all you have time for is to get superficial descriptions of the ten people. You have half an hour to make your decision. Then you will have to go to your own shelter.

So, you now have a half hour to decide which four of the ten will have to be eliminated from the shelter. Before you begin, we want to impress upon you two important considerations. It is entirely possible that the six people you choose to stay in the shelter might be the only six people left to start the human race over again. This choice is therefore very important. Try to make the best choices possible. If you do not make a choice in a half hour, then you are, in fact, choosing to let the ten people fight it out among themselves, with the possibility that more than four might perish. You have *exactly* one half hour. Here is all you know about the ten people:

1. Bookkeeper; thirty-one years old
2. His wife; six months pregnant
3. Black militant; second-year medical student
4. Famous historian-author; forty-two years old
5. Hollywood starlet; singer, dancer
6. Biochemist
7. Rabbi; fifty-four years old

8. Olympic athlete; all sports
9. Woman college student
10. Policeman with gun (they cannot be separated)

To use this strategy in a family or group setting, the leader divides the family or group members into smaller groups of three to six members and reads the procedures to them with the additional instruction that *they must decide together on a single list.*

The leader gives fifteen-, ten-, five- and one-minute warnings and then stops the groups exactly after a half hour.

Then the leader asks the participants to try to disregard the content of the activity and to examine the process and the values implications. He/she asks questions like: "How well did you listen to the others in your group?" "Did you allow yourself to be pressured into changing your mind?" "Were you so stubborn that the group couldn't reach a decision?" "Did you feel you had the absolute right answer?" "What do your own selections say to you about your values?" These questions may be thought about or written about privately, or they may be discussed in the family or group.

▸ VARIATIONS

1. Instead of eliminating four people from the shelter, rank order, as in a Forced-Choice Ladder (Strategy Number 6, page 72), the ten candidates from the most to least desirable. (There is also nothing sacred about four. It could be three or five, for example.)
2. Instead of choosing six candidates for a remote shelter,

pick four out of the ten to accompany you to your own shelter.

3. Other problem situations may be invented. For example, three (or more) people need a heart transplant and will more than likely die in three weeks if it is not performed. However, only one operation can be performed. You are to assume the role of the doctor who will perform the operation and must make the decision of who will live.

4. The descriptions of the ten people can be changed to introduce additional values issues.

   For example:

   a. A sixteen-year-old girl of questionable IQ; a high school dropout; pregnant.

   b. The same policeman with gun; thrown off the force for police brutality (or given a community-relations award).

   c. A clergyman; seventy-five years old.

   d. A thirty-six-year-old female physician; unable to have children (or known to be a confirmed racist).

   e. A forty-six-year-old male violinist; served seven years for pushing narcotics; has been out of jail for six months.

   f. A twenty-year-old, male, black militant; no special skills.

   g. A thirty-nine-year-old former prostitute; "retired" for four years.

   h. An architect; homosexual.

   i. A twenty-six-year-old male law student.

   j. The law student's twenty-five-year-old wife; spent the last nine months in a mental hospital; still heavily sedated. They refuse to be separated.

NOTE: Some people are uncomfortable with this activity because they feel it is asking us to "play God," that is, to decide who will live or die. Others are concerned that these capsule descriptions could reinforce negative stereotypes.

Of course, not every strategy—or every one of the two thousand or so questions or examples—in this book will appeal to every reader, nor should it. We encourage you to pick and choose from these activities, and do the ones that will have the most meaning to you. If The Fallout-Shelter Problem is not your cup of tea, simply skip it and go on to another.

However, having said that, we would argue that an activity like this one is a very appropriate one for people to explore and clarify their values. The fact is, in our wealthy society, we make decisions about who shall live and who shall die all the time. When we, as individuals, purchase a second television set or take our family out to a nice restaurant, we might instead use that same amount of money to keep one or more of the world's starving people alive for another year. Consciously or not, we make life-and-death value decisions like that every day or week. Whether the United States decides to retain or reform its current health care system, either decision will determine, by the thousands, who will live and who will die. And, of course, hospitals make decisions every day about when to give or deny treatment based on ability to pay, type of insurance, and other factors. So The Fallout-Shelter Problem is not completely hypothetical but reveals real value issues and priorities in our lives and belief systems.

And, in our experience, rather than reinforce stereotypes, The Fallout-Shelter Problem leads to extremely lively discussions in which participants readily identify and challenge one another's stereotypes and unquestioned assumptions. During the discussion period following the first part of the activity, a not uncommon reaction of participants is: "You know, I was so sure of my initial responses; I didn't realize there were other perspectives that also might be valid when considering these issues."

Cave-In Simulation*

► **PURPOSE**

This simulation activity encourages you to think about two important, and sometimes very scary, values issues: "What do I want to get out of life?" and "What do I have to contribute to my world?"

► **PROCEDURE**

Sit in one corner of your room, on the floor, if possible. Turn out the lights and pull down all the shades. Put a lighted candle in the center of the room. Imagine that with friends you are on an outing to some nearby caves and you have been trapped hundreds of feet below the ground by a cave-in. Twenty-four hours have passed and the air is starting to feel a bit thin for lack of oxygen. You believe, you hope, you hear the sounds of rescue workers in the far distance, but you are not certain about that and have no idea if they will reach you in time.

One of your friends comments, "I have so much to live

---

*Thanks to Larry Krafft for the basic idea for this activity.

for." Another says, "Me, too. I have so much yet to do." Then another says, "You know, we don't have anything else to do while we wait. Maybe we could keep our spirits up by talking about what we have to live for." And so everyone falls silent and thinks about the question. Now it is your turn to answer:

What do you have to live for? What do you have yet to get out of life that is important? Or considered in a different way: What do you have to contribute to the world that you would like the chance to contribute?

If you are doing this activity by yourself, write out your answer to this profound question in your Values Journal (Strategy Number 17, page 130). Take as much space to write about it as you wish.

To use this activity in a family or group setting, the leader, if the group is large, divides the family or group into small groups of four to six members. Again, the leader can ask the group(s) to bunch together in a corner of the room and turn out the lights to create the feeling of the cave-in. He/she then reads the instructions above to the group.

After people have had time to think about or write their responses, the leader asks each member of the family or group to take a turn and read what they wrote or talk about what they have to live for.

NOTE: This can be a very powerful activity when done as a group or family. It will work only if there is good deal of trust in the group and they have done other values-clarifying activities or nonjudgmental discussions together. If it is done too soon or before the trust level is established, they will avoid seriously entering into the simulation, or they will answer only superficially.

Alligator River*

► **PURPOSE**

In this strategy, you reveal some of your values by the way you react to the characters in the story. Later on, in examining your reactions to the characters, you will become more aware of your own attitudes.

► **PROCEDURE**

Read the X-rated story of Alligator River (see below), or if children are participating read the G-rated version. Following the story, rank the five characters from the most offensive character to the least objectionable. The character whom you find most reprehensible is first on the list; then the second most reprehensible, and so on, with the fifth being the least objectionable.

Then ask yourself these thought-provoking questions about the character you ranked as most offensive: "Is this the kind of person *you* least want to be like?" "What kind

---

*The authors first heard a version of this story from Rose Ann Lowe of Akron, Ohio, who attributed it to The David Frost Show.

of person would be the opposite of this character?" Write a description in your Values Journal (Strategy Number 17, page 130). List three things you could do or are now doing to be like the opposite of the person you rated as worst.

To use in a family or group, the leader divides the larger group into smaller groups of three to six members. He/she reads the procedures and then the appropriate version of the story.

After the participants have made their own rankings, they share their thinking, discuss all the pros and cons with one another, and try to reach a consensus.

Following the discussion, the leader might ask voting questions (see Strategy Number 3, page 25) to find out how participants ranked each of the characters. (For example, "How many felt Abigail was the best character? How many felt she was the worst character?")

The Alligator River Story

Rated "X":
Once upon a time there was a woman named Abigail who was in love with a man named Gregory. Gregory lived on the shore of a river. Abigail lived on the opposite shore of the river. The river that separated the two lovers was teeming with man-eating alligators. Abigail wanted to cross the river to be with Gregory. Unfortunately, the bridge had been washed out. So she went to ask Sinbad, a riverboat captain, to take her across. He said he would be glad to if she would consent to go to bed with him preceding the voyage. She promptly refused and went to a friend named Ivan to explain her plight. Ivan did not want to be involved at all in the situation. Abigail felt her only alternative was to accept Sinbad's terms. Sinbad fulfilled

his promise to Abigail and delivered her into the arms of Gregory.

When she told Gregory about her amorous escapade in order to cross the river, Gregory cast her aside with disdain. Heartsick and dejected, Abigail turned to Slug with her tail of woe. Slug, feeling compassion for Abigail, sought out Gregory and beat him brutally. Abigail was happy to see Gregory getting his due. As the sun sets on the horizon, we hear Abigail laughing at Gregory.

Rated "G":
Once there was a girl named Abigail who was in love with a boy named Gregory. Gregory had an unfortunate mishap and broke his glasses. Abigail, being a true friend, volunteered to take them to be repaired. But the repair shop was across the river, and during a flash flood the bridge was washed away. Poor Gregory could see nothing without his glasses, so Abigail was desperate to get across the river to the repair shop.

While she was standing forlornly on the bank of the river, clutching the broken glasses in her hands, a boy named Sinbad glided by in a rowboat. She asked Sinbad if he would take her across. He agreed to on condition that while she was having the glasses repaired, she would go to a nearby store and steal a transistor radio that he had been wanting. Abigail refused to do this and went to a friend named Ivan who had a boat.

When Abigail told Ivan her problem, he said he was too busy to help her out and didn't want to be involved. Abigail, feeling that she had no other choice, returned to Sinbad and told him she would agree to his plan.

When Abigail returned the repaired glasses to Gregory, she told him what she had to do. Gregory was appalled at what she had done and told her he never wanted to see her again.

Abigail, upset, turned to Slug with her tale of woe. Slug was so sorry for Abigail that he promised her he would get even with Gregory. They went to the school playground where Gregory was playing ball, and Abigail watched happily while Slug beat Gregory up and broke his glasses again.

NOTE: In a family or group setting, this strategy often generates a good deal of emotional involvement. Participants may attempt to attack and criticize each other's rankings. If listening to others or intolerance toward others' ideas proves to be a problem, the leader can use Values-Focus Game rules (Strategy Number 18, page 132) or Rogerian Listening (Strategy Number 51, page 234).

Rogerian Listening

▶ PURPOSE

Part of the valuing process is considering alternatives. To be open to alternatives we must be able to really listen to other people. According to Dr. Carl Rogers, good listening involves:

1. Not only hearing the words of the speaker, but hearing the feelings behind the words as well.
2. Empathizing with the speaker; that is, feeling his/her feelings and seeing the world through the speaker's eyes.
3. Suspending one's own value judgments so as to understand the speaker's thoughts and feelings as the speaker experiences them.

This strategy teaches you to really listen. You learn that communication is a two-way street. You will begin to understand how difficult it is really to listen to another person, especially if you disagree with him or her, and you will come to realize how much of normal conversation is really talking *at* rather than *with* one another.

► PROCEDURE

This listening exercise is to be used in a family or group setting and is done in groups of three or more participants. One person serves as monitor, the others as discussants. The monitor helps the discussants find a subject of mutual interest, but one on which the discussants have different views or feelings. The first discussant states his or her position on the issue and a discussion follows.

In the typical discussion, we are so concerned with what we are going to say next, or so involved with planning our response, that we often tune out or miss the full meaning of what is being said. In this exercise, before any discussant offers his or her own point of view, he or she must summarize the essence of the previous speaker's statement so that the previous speaker honestly feels his or her statement has been understood. It is the monitor's role to see that this process takes place. *Here is an example:*

FRED:	. . . and that's why I'm in favor of a guaranteed, minimum annual income.
JERRY:	Okay. You're saying you favor the guaranteed income because you think it will break the cycle of people staying on welfare and because it will put more money in circulation and thus create more jobs. Is that right?
FRED:	You got it.
JERRY:	Okay. But I think just the opposite would happen. You'd have people knowing they'd get a decent wage if they didn't work so . . .
FRAN:	But that's ridiculous. Why would . . .
MONITOR:	Hold it, Fran. Hold it. First of all, Jerry didn't finish his point. Second of all, you didn't restate it before responding.

FRAN: Sorry.

JERRY: Well, my point was, if somebody thinks he doesn't have to work and he'll get paid anyway, then why should he work?

FRAN: Well, I'll tell you. He'll work because . . .

MONITOR: Hold it, again. What did Jerry say?

FRAN: Oh, yeah. Jerry's worried this won't work. But I think . . .

MONITOR: Wait a minute. Jerry, are you satisfied that Fran understands your argument?

JERRY: No.

MONITOR: Fran, do you want to try it again? Or do you want Jerry to repeat his point?

This exercise can last as long as the groups seem interested and involved in their discussions. Every now and then, the leader asks the monitor to change roles with one of the discussants.

The exercise can be followed by I Learned Statements (Strategy Number 15, page 126) or by a discussion about listening.

NOTE: When tempers flare, when tension rises, when parents and children, managers and workers, different races, or any group of people stop listening to one another, this listening exercise can reduce conflict and facilitate communication.

The Free-Choice Game*

▸ **PURPOSE**

We frequently are in situations in which another person shares with us a choice that he or she is considering:

"I'm thinking about buying a new car."

"I can't decide whether to cut my hair or not."

"I have a really good job offer, but I have mixed feelings about accepting it."

"I don't know how to make up with my friend after our fight."

"I think I'd like to work for a year—you know, be on my own for a while—before going to college."

If the decision the person finally makes is to be of value to him or her, if it is to be a viable decision the person can be comfortable with and succeed in carrying out, it must be one that he or she has freely chosen, after thoughtful consideration of the alternatives. There is a

*Thanks to Saville Sax and the NEXTEP Program, Southern Illinois University for this strategy.

time to give people the wisdom of your thinking and experience. But there is a time to help others find their own wisdom.

This activity helps you become the kind of listener who can help a person make his or her own choice. It teaches you an effective way of helping others make difficult values choices. It also sharpens your ability to listen fully to another person.

▶ **PROCEDURE**

The leader introduces the game. The game can be played with three or more family members or people in a group, but five or six in a group is usually maximally productive. One person is the focus person, one is the monitor, and the rest are the helpers.

The focus person is a volunteer who has a life choice that he or she would like to discuss with a small group of good listeners. The helpers' job is to help the focus person make his or her own best choice. They do this by asking questions. They may not make a statement unless they first ask permission of the focus person. Generally, their questions follow a five-step progression:

1. Understanding. They ask questions to gain enough information so they feel they have a good understanding of the focus person's choice dilemma.

2. Clarifying. They ask thought-provoking questions to test out some of their own hypotheses and to help the focus person think more deeply about his or her situation.

3. Exploring alternatives. They inquire about what alternatives the focus person sees open to him or her.

With permission, they suggest other alternatives the focus person might want to consider.

4. Exploring consequences. They ask questions that cause the focus person to explore the pros and cons and consequences of the alternatives open to him or her.

5. Exploring feelings and choosing. They ask questions that encourage the focus person to explore his or her feelings about the alternatives and their consequences, and to think about what choice he or she is leaning toward at that point.

This format is not inflexible. Groups will naturally jump back and forth among the five stages of decision making. But, in general, this structure seems to work. If the focus person first feels understood, he or she will be more open to clarifying questions. And before choosing, all the alternatives and their consequences have to be explored.

The focus person is in control and can end the game at any time. He or she can and should tell the helpers when feeling pressured by their questions—if, for example, the focus person feels they are trying to persuade him or her toward a given choice.

The monitor's job is to encourage the group to follow the five-step process in case they are putting the cart before the horse. ("I think we are exploring alternatives before fully understanding the choice situation. Focus person, are you satisfied that we understand your dilemma?") The monitor also steps in when people are making statements disguised as questions, (e.g., "Don't you feel it would be wiser to . . ."). The game goes on for about a half hour to forty minutes. At any point, the monitor might ask the focus person whether the helpers are following the rules or are trying to impose their views on him or her. At the end, the monitor asks the focus person to share any insights gained with the group or say if he or she is any closer to a choice.

NOTE: The leader encourages the participants to pose actual *choices* with which they are confronted rather than *problems* they face. If the focus person raises a problem per se (lack of confidence, guilt feelings about a parental relationship, dislike of one's physical appearance), then the helpers are put in the position of being psychoanalysts, for which they are not equipped. But if the focus person presents a choice situation (whether or not to ask her for a date, how much to spend on a child's birthday present, whether or not to dye his hair), then the groups can play a meaningful role.

STRATEGY NUMBERS 53 THROUGH 59*

NOTE: *The next seven strategies (Numbers 53–59) can be treated as independent activities. However, they are most effective when treated as a seven-part exercise. This is a serious and important group of activities that focus on death as well as life and are, for some people, in a high-risk category. However, the impact on many people is powerful and positive.*

The entire sequence can easily take two hours. You can do them all at once or piecemeal over short time periods. Pencil or pen and paper are required. Silence and space for privacy are important.

This sequence of activities can be done individually or they can be done in a trusting family or group setting. When done with others, each family or group member first does the activity individually. Then each person who wishes to may share his or her responses and feelings from the activity with the group.

---

*We had used five of these seven strategies for many years. Later we came across Phil Doster's summation of Herb Shepard's "Life Planning Project" and discovered that he too used many of the same strategies. We have borrowed the "Lifeline" and the "Two Ideal Days" from Dr. Shepard, as well as his ordering of the exercises. Later on, we were told that Arthur Shedlin used a similar approach many years before any of us, which illustrates how many of the strategies in this book have been in the public domain for years and, like folk songs, will continue to be passed on and adapted time and again.

STRATEGY 53

Lifeline

► PURPOSE

This simple strategy confronts you with the reality of life
and death and sets the tone for the next six strategies. It
implicitly conveys the concept "I have just so many years
left and I have a choice as to how I will spend those years."

► PROCEDURE

Draw a horizontal line across your paper. Put a dot at each
end of the line. Over the left dot, put the number zero.
This dot represents your birth. Write your birth date under
this dot. The dot on your right represents your ultimate
death. How long do you believe you will live? At what age
do you think you'll die? Over the right dot, put a number
that indicates your best guess as to how many years you
will live. Write your estimated year of death under the
right dot.

Now place a dot that represents where you are right now
on the line between birth and death. Write today's date
under this dot.

This diagram is your lifeline. Look at it, study it, and think about it. Let it really settle into your consciousness.

After a minute or two of meditation time, answer the question "How did you feel and what did you think as you looked at your lifeline?" Write about your reaction in your Values Journal (Strategy Number 17, page 130).

STRATEGY 54

Who Are You?

▶ **PURPOSE**

This exercise calls attention to the many hats we wear in life and shows how we often allow ourselves to be defined merely by the roles we have been assigned. It also opens up alternatives to consider for the criteria by which we judge ourselves.

▶ **PROCEDURE**

Imagine that you have been called before a congressional investigating committee, Saint Peter, or another august interviewer who asks you to testify and answer the question "Who are you?" When you answer, they again ask, "Who are you?" (Or "And in addition, who are you?" or "Who else are you?") This process continues until the question has been asked ten times or more.

Answer the question "Who are you?" at least ten times or until you run out of answers. Write down your answers.

If you are doing this activity by yourself, then consult several friends and family members. Ask them if they will answer the question "Who am I?" That is, they are to answer by telling you who you are or how they see you. Then ask, "Who else am I?" and so on. Record their answers. Then compare your responses with theirs. Note any similarities or differences.

NOTE: If you are doing this as part of the sequence of strategies 53 to 59 with your family or group, it is better not to get feedback from others at this point because it will probably interfere with the quiet, introspective nature of this life-planning sequence. However, asking one another "Who am I?" could be another, valuable activity to do at a later time.

Epitaph

▶ **PURPOSE**

Sometimes it helps to gain perspective on life by contemplating death. What is life all about? What difference would it make if you were not alive? This strategy has us look at the meaning of our lives in a simple but challenging way.

▶ **PROCEDURE**

Have you ever been to old graveyards and read some of the inscriptions on the tombstones? For example:

"Here lies Mary Smith. She had so much love to give."
"Sarah Miller, A Woman of Valor."
"Ezra Jones lived as he died. Out of debt, out of sight, and out of sorts."

What would you want engraved on your own tombstone? What would be an accurate description of you and your life in a few short words? When you have an answer, write it down.

On a new piece of paper, draw a tombstone (or if you wish, get some construction paper and cut it in the shape of a tombstone) and put your epitaph on it, complete with stonecutter-type illustrations or decorations. File it in your Values Journal (Strategy Number 17, page 130).

If you wish, consult *Bartlett's Quotations* or old yearbooks to choose appropriate statements for your epitaph.

Here are our epitaphs:

Leland Howe: "Some men see things as they are and say, 'Why?' I dreamed of things that never were and said, 'Why not?' "

Howie Kirschenbaum: "He cared."

Sid Simon: "Searcher, teacher, giver. And needing, wanting, loving, and sometimes crying."

Obituary

▶ PURPOSE

This strategy helps you see your life more clearly from the perspective of your imagined death. It raises specific issues about the quality of one's life. It reinforces the fact that we still have a life ahead of us to do whatever we want to with.

▶ PROCEDURE

You are going to look at life by viewing it again from the perspective of death by writing out your own obituary. Here is a simple format, although you are free to write your obituary in your own form. You can use as many of these suggestions as you wish or add your own.

James Clark, age forty-five, died yesterday from . . .

He was a member . . .

He is survived by . . .

At the time of his death he was working on becoming . . .

He will be remembered for . . .

He will be mourned by . . . because . . .

The world will suffer the loss of his contributions in the areas of . . .

He always wanted, but he never got to . . .

The body will be . . .

Flowers may be sent . . .

In lieu of flowers . . .

▶ **VARIATION**

Draw a line right down the middle of your paper. On the left side, write your obituary as it would appear in the newspaper if you were to die today. On the right side, write your obituary as you would like it to appear in the newspaper if you were to die three years hence. Or write it as you would like it to appear in the newspaper after you lived your life to its full end.

Two Ideal Days

▸ PURPOSE

As part of the life-planning series, this strategy makes the point that we ought to be clear about what we want out of life. You are asked to construct two perfect days, and in the process, learn more about what you really love in life.

▸ PROCEDURE

Project yourself into the future, any time from tomorrow to several years from now, and imagine two days that would be ideal for you. Imagine forty-eight hours of what for you would be the best possible use of that period of time. You can fantasize whatever you want; the only limit is the time limit of forty-eight hours.

Write about your perfect, ideal two days: where you would be, what you would be doing, who else might be there, and so on. Try to picture what you would be doing for the full forty-eight hours. Go into as much detail as you can picture in your fantasy—smells, sounds, the weather, if they play a part.

I Learned Statements (Strategy Number 15, page 126) are a good follow-up to this exercise.

Life Inventory

▶ **PURPOSE**

This exercise asks you to look at some of the major themes and events of your life. In the life-planning sequence, it ties together the previous exercises and moves you away from the fantasy level toward past and present realities.

▶ **PROCEDURE**

Answer the following questions in writing. Try to write a few sentences about each question.

1. What was the happiest year or period in your life?
2. What things do you do well?
3. Write about a turning point in your life.
4. What has been the lowest point in your life?
5. Was there an event in which you demonstrated great courage?
6. Was there a time of heavy grief? More than one?
7. What are some things you would like to stop doing?
8. What are some things you would really like to get better at?

9. Write about some peak experience you have had.

10. Write about some peak experiences you would like to have.

11. Are there some values you are struggling to establish?

12. Write about one missed opportunity in your life.

13. What are some things you want to start doing now, right at this point in your life?

Self-Contracts

► PURPOSE

It is one thing to talk about wanting something in life and another thing to do something about getting it. This strategy attempts to close the gap between what we want and what we are doing to achieve it.

This strategy can follow any values activity that generates feelings about how we live our lives. When we are seriously thinking about the quality of our lives, this is the best time for self-contracts. Thus, it is a natural conclusion to the preceding series of exercises.

► PROCEDURE

In this activity, you are going to make a contract with yourself about some change you would like to make in your life. It can involve starting something new, stopping something old, or changing some present aspect of your life.

For example, perhaps you want to do something more about conservation. You might make a self-contract that says: "For the next week, I will turn out the lights each and every time I leave a room, thus saving electricity, thus cutting down on the pollution from the electric company." Perhaps you want to save for your child's college education and will contract to save $50 a week until she is eighteen. Perhaps you will contract that every time you get angry with a particular person you will tell him how it makes you feel when he does such and such instead of simply yelling at him. Make the contract about any area in your life that is important to you and that you would like to work on.

Then write out your contract. Finally, if you really intend to carry out the contract, sign your name at the bottom.

A week or so later, take time to review how well you have been doing in carrying out your contract.

NOTE: One problem people often run into is that they make grandiose contracts that there is almost no hope of ever carrying out. So try to be specific and realistic, and make a contract that can be completed in the near future.

Ready for Summer (Strategy Number 71, page 291), Getting Started (Strategy Number 28, page 164), and Removing Barriers to Action (Strategy Number 27, page 162) are all variations of self-contracts.

A comment from one of our students might help demonstrate the importance of self-contracts. "As far as self-contracts go, I usually don't like making them, but I've broken down and made one. I'm a hostess-cashier and the management is very adamant about greeting all the customers—something I never do because I feel false when I do it. However, tonight I've decided to give it a try, to see if I can become comfortable doing it through simple repetition."

In other words, until we make a personal commitment to act in a certain way or to demonstrate a particular value, we are less likely to take the action or live the value.

How Would Your Life Be Different?

► PURPOSE

Remember the TV programs *The Millionaire, Superman,* and *Run for Your Life* or the movie *Aladdin*. Each of them was quite a success, and each appealed to the same basic fantasy: "How would my life be different if . . . ?"

This strategy uses these fantasies and others to help you think more deeply about some of your hopes and aspirations, and about what you are doing to achieve them.

► PROCEDURE

Imagine that you have just been informed by your doctor that you have only one year left to live. You believe that her diagnosis is absolutely accurate. Describe in writing how your life during the next year would be different if you were to receive this news.

After you have had time to think and write on this question, answer the following question: "If I want to change my life in some way, what's stopping me from moving in that direction now?"

▶ OTHER EXAMPLES

1. How would my life be different if someone handed me a bona fide, tax-free gift of one million dollars?
2. How would my life be different if I had the powers of Superman?
3. How would my life be different if I had a genie who could transform my appearance in whatever way I desire?
4. How would my life be different if I were to become president of the United States?

NOTE: Look for the values indicators behind your fantasies. For example, let's say you would like to be Superman so you could fly. Ask yourself, "Why would I want to do that?" You answer, "So I could feel free like a bird." We would say, "So you value freedom?" You agree. Then ask yourself, "Am I doing anything now that makes me feel free or that is working toward this goal?"

STRATEGY 61

What Is Important—A Song*

► **PURPOSE**

For all of us, the question "What is important?" represents a lifelong search. This song, originally designed for children, is an enjoyable and useful way to encourage yourself to think about what you regard as important in life.

► **PROCEDURE**

Play the simple song below on guitar or piano, or sing it without musical accompaniment. Then sing it again, and when you reach the line "Tell me if you know," say something you feel is important. Continue the song until you run out of ideas.

Record your responses in your Values Journal (Strategy Number 17, page 130). Data collected at different times is very useful as you look for trends in your life.

To use this strategy in a family or group, the group sings the song and when they reach the line "Tell me if you

---

*Words and music by Marianne Preger-Simon

know," anyone who wants to contributes something he or she feels is important.

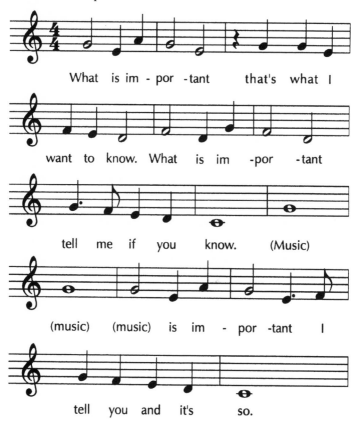

What is im - por -tant   that's what I want to know. What is im -por - tant tell me if you know. (Music) (music) (music) is im - por -tant I tell you and it's so.

▶ **VARIATIONS**

The leader can ask people to think of what their families, people in the news, or historical or literary characters might say is important. Substitute these names for "I" in the line "I tell you and it's so."

I Am Proud—A Song*

► **PURPOSE**

The I Am Proud song is used to elicit statements of prizing and cherishing. It is a musical version of Proud Statements and Whips (Strategy Number 11, page 103).

► **PROCEDURE**

Play the song below on a guitar or piano, or sing it without musical accompaniment. When you come to the line "and I'll tell you," answer by saying something that you are proud of having done.

To use the strategy in a family or group setting, all sing together. When you come to "and I'll tell you," one person tells of something he or she is proud of having done. The song is repeated as often as is desirable at the time, with many or even all members

---

*Words and music by Marianne Preger-Simon.

getting a chance to tell something they are proud of having done.

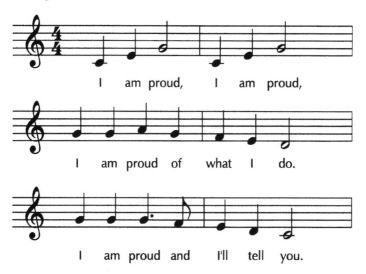

> I am proud, I am proud,
>
> I am proud of what I do.
>
> I am proud and I'll tell you.

► **VARIATIONS**

Narrow the topic to one of the areas of confusion and conflict, e.g., tell about something you are proud of in relation to money, work/school, or family.

The song can tell of being proud of other people by changing the words to: ". . . I am proud of you know who; I am proud and I'll tell you."

What's in Your Wallet?

► PURPOSE

We can learn a lot about what we value by looking more closely at some aspects of our lives we never thought were very important or had values implications. Looking at what we carry in our wallets or on our person illustrates this point.

► PROCEDURE

Take out three things from your wallet or purse that show three different things you value. These three items can be anything at all; the mere fact that you carry them in your wallet says something. Then think about what any or all of them mean to you and your value system. Write down your thoughts.

Follow up the exercise with I Learned Statements (Strategy Number 15, page 126).

In a family or group setting, go around the group or divide large groups into smaller groups of five or six—and give each person a chance to say something about his or her life and values as evidenced by the items he or she carries, day in and out, in his or her wallet.

NOTE: If you do not carry a wallet or purse, choose items from your pockets or handbags, backpacks, or even notebooks.

Clothes and Values*

▶ **PURPOSE**

Whether we like it or not, our clothes often tell other people something about our values. It would seem important for us to know what messages we send through the clothes we wear and to look at whether or not these are the messages we do in fact want to communicate. This strategy begins this process.

The exercise advances the notion that often we do something hoping that it will have one specific effect while in reality it has quite another effect. We don't dress completely unconsciously, although some of us work a lot harder at making a statement with our clothes than others.

▶ **PROCEDURE**

On a sheet of paper, draw the following chart:

---

*This is adapted from an exercise the authors first learned from Jerry Weinstein.

Item of clothing	What I *want* my clothing to say about me	What my clothing *does* say about me
1. Shirt or blouse		
2. Slacks, skirt, etc.		
3. Shoes		
4. Sweater, sport jacket, etc.		
5. Watch or other jewelry on wrist or hands		
6.		
7.		
8.		

In the first column, you are to list, in some detail, the clothing you are actually wearing at this time. Try to list each and every *visible* item, for example, each piece of jewelry.

What we wear often tells something about our values. We often make statements with our clothes. Ask yourself, "What do I want to say about myself with what I picked out to wear today?" Some examples might be: "I want to appear very 'cool.'" Or "I want people to know I'm prosperous." Or "I want men to know I have shapely legs." Or "I want to convey a considered sloppiness." Or "I want my muscles to show." Be as frank as you can and try not to be defensive as you fill in the second column. Later you will get a chance to check out with other people how they see you and what you convey to them by what you are wearing today.

If you do not think you have anything to convey through

some aspects of your clothing, leave those spaces blank. You can still find out what you *do* convey to others by those aspects of your dress. And if several categories of dress all contribute to one effect for you, group these together in some way.

Then consult several friends and family members (or, if you're feeling brave, coworkers or acquaintances) and ask them to fill in the third column. Cover up the second column by taping paper over it before filling in the third column. Impressions should be recorded without comment.

Then uncover the second column and check to see what, if any, are the differences between what you wanted to convey and what you actually did convey.

Save your chart in the Values Journal or the Values Data Bank (Strategy Number 17, page 130).

NOTE: Remember that feedback from only several others cannot be considered a fair sample of the way everyone views the way we dress.

▸ VARIATIONS

There are other things that can be surveyed in the same way. For example: List six prominent things in a room, at home, or in your office. What do you *want* them to say about you when someone enters the room? What do these six things *actually* say about you to people who have been in that room or office? Or what are five things you have written on the covers of your schoolbooks? What do you want them to say about you? What *do* they say to other people?

The Suitcase Strategy

► **PURPOSE**

The goal of this strategy is to have you assess the relative value of your personal possessions.

► **PROCEDURE**

Pretend that you are going on a very long voyage across the ocean to a new land. Choosing one of the examples below, briefly review what you may expect to find upon arriving in the new land. You can take with you only one large suitcase, since the boat going over will be very crowded. Anything you cannot put in the suitcase will have to be left behind. Now take out a sheet of paper and make a list of the things you will want to take.

When you have completed your list, identify and write down your reasons for the choices you made. Also write about whether you are proud of or feel good about the choices you made during this activity.

Save your list in The Values Journal or Values Data Bank (Strategy Number 17, page 130).

To use in a family or group setting, have each member share his or her list with other family or group members.

The New Land

The kind of information you have about the new land you are going to can influence your decision about what to pack. For instance, survival items might become more of a consideration in an unsettled or underdeveloped area than in a land of plenty.

Here are three sample descriptions of the new land:

1. This land is largely agricultural. There are a few small towns, but most of the people live and work on farms. The climate is very similar to that in the northeastern United States. The countryside is beautiful, with many mountains and lakes.
2. This land is very poor and primitive, but it has been strongly influenced by its former British rulers and it is very formal in its dress and customs. The climate is tropical all year round. Most of the people live in grass huts, but the ruling class live luxuriously and the hotels have first-class facilities.
3. This is a bustling, cosmopolitan resort center. People come here for their holidays from all over the world. Anything and everything is available at a price.

► VARIATIONS

1. Repeat the activity for the other two lands described above. Reflect and write about how your lists were similar or different for the three different lands. Make I Learned Statements (Strategy Number 15, page 126) about your observations.

2. Choose a land you wish to or plan to visit or revisit.

3. Assume you are going to emigrate to a country and setting much like your own. Forget about survival issues; assume your tools and essentials will be provided or can be purchased. Focus on your personal possessions and list which of your clothes, books, photographs, records, or other personal items are so important to you that you would include them in your single, large suitcase. Then look at your list and write or talk about what your list tells you about your life priorities and values.

STRATEGY 66

The Miracle Workers*

▸ **PURPOSE**

This strategy poses a problem that confronts you with many attractive alternatives to choose from. It helps you get in touch with your feelings about what is important to you.

▸ **PROCEDURE**

Using the following worksheet, which contains the names of fifteen miracle workers, choose the five miracle workers you value the highest, that is, the five whose gifts you would most like to receive. Then pick five more names. This leaves five miracle workers in the least desirable group.

Then see if you can discover any patterns. Some helpful questions are: "What seems to link together the five most desirable people and what joins the five least desirable to me?" "What values am I demonstrating in my choices?" "Are there any choices that somehow seem out of place

---

*Developed by Mark Phillips

with the others in that grouping?" Write down your answers.

Then ask yourself this difficult question: "What are you now doing to achieve what your top five miracle workers could do for you?" Make a list in your Values Journal (Strategy Number 17, page 130) of what you are doing or could do.

Finally, do a Self-Contract (Strategy Number 59, page 254) based on your learnings from this exercise. The implication is that each of us is a miracle worker. What miracles do we want to strive for? Where do we begin? How can we help each other?

To use in a family or group, have each person share his or her choices and responses to the above questions.

▶ **WORKSHEET**

A group of fifteen experts, considered miracle workers by those who use their services, have agreed to provide these services to you. Their extraordinary skills are guaranteed to be 100 percent effective. It is up to you to decide which of these people can best provide you with what you want.

The experts are:

1. **Dr. Dorian Grey**—A noted plastic surgeon, she can make you look exactly as you want to look by means of a new painless technique. (She also uses hormones to alter body structures and size!) Your ideal physical appearance can be a reality.

2. **Baron VonBarrons**—A college-placement and job-placement expert. The job or college of your choice, in the location of your choice, will be yours!

3. **Jedediah Methuselah**—Guarantees you long life (to

the age of 200) with your aging process slowed down proportionately. For example, at the age of sixty you will look and feel like twenty-five.

4. **Drs. Masters Johnson and Fanny Hill**—Experts in the area of sexual relations, they guarantee that you will be the perfect male or female, will enjoy sex, and will bring pleasure to others.

5. **Dr. Yin Yang**—An organismic expert, she will provide you with perfect health and protection from physical injury throughout your life.

6. **Dr. Sister Brothers**—An expert in dealing with parents and children, she guarantees that you will never have any family problems again. You will be free from family conflicts and your family will be happy together.

7. **Rev. I.M.N. Heaven**—Following his advice will surely lead to spiritual enlightenment and salvation.

8. **"Pop" U Larity**—He guarantees that you will have the friends you want now and in the future. You will find it easy to approach those you like and they will find you easily approachable.

9. **Dr. Samantha Smart**—She will develop your common sense and your intelligence to a level in excess of 150 I.Q. It will remain at this level through your entire lifetime.

10. **Rocky Fellah**—Wealth will be yours, with guaranteed schemes for earning millions within weeks.

11. **Dwight D. DeGawl**—This world-famed leadership expert will train you quickly. You will be listened to, looked up to, and respected by those around you.

12. **Dr. Close Encounters**—You will be well liked by all and will never be lonely. A life filled with love and intimacy will be yours.

13. **Dr. Claire Voyant**—All of your questions about the future will be answered, continually, through the training of this soothsayer.

14. **Dr. Hinnah Self**—She guarantees that you will have self-knowledge, self-liking, self-respect, and self-confidence. True self-assurance will be yours.

15. **Prof. Val U. Clear**—With her help, you will always know what you want and you will be completely clear on all the cloudy issues of these confused days.

Ways to Live

► PURPOSE

This strategy asks you to formulate your own philosophy of life by responding to thirteen ways to live. It leads to the consideration of alternative lifestyles and causes you to more thoroughly consider your own lifestyle.

► PROCEDURE

Read over the Ways-to-Live worksheet that follows and rate each item using the rating scale provided. Then rank order all thirteen choices, from your first preference to your last.

Write out your own way-to-live statement, reflecting your own philosophy of life at this point in your life. You can borrow phrases or sentences from any of the thirteen described here or create your own wording and ideas.

Finally, you are to think of ten things you have done in the last week that are consistent with the philosophy of life or the way to live that you have just described. This bridges the gap between a general philosophical statement and the way you actually live.

I Wonder Statements (Strategy Number 16, page 128) are a good conclusion to this thought-provoking exercise.

► WORKSHEET

Ways to Live*

Instructions: Below are described thirteen ways to live that various persons, at various times, have advocated and followed.

You are to write numbers in the margin to indicate how much you yourself like or dislike each of these ways to live. Do them in order, one after the other.

Remember that it is not a question of what kind of life you now lead, the kind of life you think it prudent to live in our society, or the kind of life you think would be good for other persons, but simply the kind of life you personally would like to live.

Use the following scale and write one of these numbers in the margin alongside each of the ways to live:

7. I like it *very* much
6. I like it *quite* a lot
5. I like it *slightly*
4. I am *indifferent* to it
3. I dislike it *slightly*
2. I dislike it *quite* a lot
1. I dislike it *very much*

Way 1: In this design for living the individual actively participates in the social life of his/her community, not

---

*Reproduced with permission of the author. Questionnaire from Charles Morris, *Varieties of Human Value* (Chicago: University of Chicago Press, 1956), pp. 15–19. Slight adaptations have been made to the original text to adapt it for this exercise.

primarily to change it but to understand, appreciate, and preserve the best that humankind has attained. In this lifestyle, excessive desires are avoided and moderation is sought. One wants the good things of life, but in an orderly way. Life is to have clarity, balance, refinement, and control. Vulgarity, great enthusiasm, irrational behavior, impatience, and indulgence are to be avoided. Friendship is to be esteemed, but not easy intimacy with many people. Life is marked by discipline, intelligibility, good manners, and predictability. Social changes are to be made slowly and carefully, so that what has been achieved in human culture is not lost. The individual is active physically and socially, but not in a hectic or radical way. Restraint and intelligence should give order to an active life.

Way 2: In this way of life, the individual for the most part goes it alone, assuring oneself of privacy in living quarters, having much time to oneself, attempting to control his/her own life. Emphasis is on self-sufficiency, reflection and meditation, knowledge of oneself. Intimate associations and relationships with social groups are to be avoided, as are the physical manipulation of objects and attempts at control of the physical environment. One should aim to simplify one's external life, to moderate desires that depend upon physical and social forces outside of oneself. One concentrates on refinement, clarification, and self-direction. Not much is to be gained by living outwardly. One must avoid dependence upon persons or things; the center of life should be found within oneself.

Way 3: This way of life makes central the sympathetic concern for other persons. Affection is the main thing in life, affection that is free from all traces of the imposition of oneself upon others or of using others for one's own purposes. Greed in possessions, emphasis on sexual passion, striving for power over persons and things, excessive emphasis upon intellect, and undue concern for oneself are to be avoided. These things hinder the sympathetic love among persons that alone gives significance to life. Aggressiveness blocks receptivity to the forces that foster genuine personal growth. One should purify oneself, restrain one's self-assertiveness, and become receptive, appreciative, and helpful in relating to other persons.

Way 4: Life is something to be enjoyed—sensuously enjoyed, enjoyed with relish and abandonment. The aim in life should not be to control the course of the world or to change society or the lives of others, but to be open and receptive to things and persons, and to delight in them. Life is a festival, not a workshop or a school for moral discipline. To let oneself go, to let things and persons affect oneself, is more important than to do—or to do good. Such enjoyment requires that one be self-centered enough to be keenly aware of what is happening within in order to be free for new happiness. One should avoid entanglements, should not be too dependent on particular people or things, should not be self-sacrificing; one should be alone a lot, should have time for meditation and awareness of oneself. Both solitude and sociability are necessary for the good life.

Way 5: This way of life stresses the social group rather than the individual. A person should not focus on him/herself, withdraw from people, be aloof or self-centered. Rather, one should merge oneself with a social group, enjoy cooperation and companionship, join with others in resolute activity for the realization of common goals. Persons are social and persons are active; life should merge energetic group activity and cooperative group enjoyment. Meditation, restraint, concern for one's self-sufficiency, abstract intellectuality, solitude, stress on one's possessions all cut the roots that bind persons together. One should live outwardly with gusto, enjoying the good things of life, working with others to secure the things that a pleasant and energetic social life make possible. Those who oppose this ideal are not to be dealt with too tenderly. Life can't be too fastidious.

Way 6: This philosophy sees life as dynamic and the individual as an active participant. Life continuously tends to stagnate, to become comfortable, to become sicklied over with the pale cast of thought. Against these tendencies, a person must stress the need for constant activity—physical action, adventure, the realistic solution of specific problems as they appear, the improvement of techniques for controlling the world and society. Humankind's future depends primarily on what one does, not on what one feels or on one's speculations. New problems constantly arise and always will arise. Improvements must always be made if humankind is to progress. We can't just follow the past or dream of what the future might be. We have to work resolutely and continually if control is to be gained over the forces that threaten us. One should rely on technical advances made possible by scientific knowledge. One should find one's goal in the solution of one's problems. The good is the enemy of the better.

Way 7: This philosophy says that we should, at various times and in various ways, accept something from all other paths of life but give no one our exclusive allegiance. At one moment one way may be more appropriate; at another moment another is the most appropriate. Life should contain enjoyment, action, and contemplation in about equal amounts. When any one way is carried to extremes, we lose something important for our life. So we must cultivate flexibility, admit diversity in ourselves, accept the tension this diversity produces, find a place for detachment in the midst of enjoyment and activity. The goal of life is found in the dynamic integration of enjoyment, action, and contemplation, and in the dynamic interaction of the various paths of life. One should use all of them in building a life, not one alone.

Way 8: Enjoyment should be the keynote of life—not the hectic search for intense and exciting pleasures, but the enjoyment of the simple and easily obtainable pleasures, the pleasures of just existing, of savoring food, of comfortable surroundings, of talking with friends, of rest and relaxation. A home that is warm and comfortable, chairs and a bed that are soft, a kitchen well stocked with food, a door open to friends—this is the place to live. Body at ease, relaxed, calm in its movements, not hurried, breath slow and easy, a willingness to nod and to rest, gratitude to the world that feeds the body—so should it be. Driving ambition and the fanaticism of ascetic ideals are the signs of discontented people who have lost the capacity to float in the stream of simple, carefree, wholesome enjoyment.

Way 9: Receptivity and reverence should be the keynotes of life. The good things of life come of their own accord and come unsought. They cannot be found by resolute action. They cannot be found in the indulgence of the sensuous desires of the body. They cannot be gathered by participation in the turmoil of social life. They cannot be given to others by attempts to be helpful. They cannot be garnered by hard thinking. Rather do they come unsought when the bars of the self are down. When the self has ceased to make demands and waits in quiet receptivity, it becomes open to transcendent powers that nourish it and work though it; sustained by this spiritual power, it knows joy and peace. Sitting alone under the trees and the sky, open to nature's voices, calm and receptive, prayerful and reverent, then can wisdom from without enter within.

Way 10: Self-control should be the keynote of life—not the easy self-control that retreats from the world, but the vigilant, stern, determined control of a self that lives in the world, and knows the strength of the world and the limits of human power. The good life is rationally directed and firmly pursues high ideals. It is not bent by the seductive voices of comfort and desire. It does not expect social utopia. It is distrustful of final victories. Too much should not be expected. Yet one can with vigilance hold firm the reins of self, control unruly impulses, understand one's place in the world, guide one's actions by reason, maintain self-reliant independence. And in this way, though one will finally perish, one can keep his/her human dignity and respect, and die with cosmic good manners.

Way 11: The contemplative life is the good life. The external world is not a fit habitat for humankind. It is too big, too cold, too pressing. It is the life turned inward that is rewarding. The rich internal world of ideals, of sensitive feelings, of reverie, of self-knowledge, is man's true home. By the cultivation of the self within, one becomes human. Only then does there arise deep sympathy with all that lives, an understanding of the suffering inherent in life, a realization of the futility of aggressive action, the attainment of contemplative joy. Conceit then falls away and austerity is dissolved. In giving up the world, one finds the larger and finer sea of the inner self.

Way 12: The use of the body's energy is the secret of rewarding life. The hands need material to make into something; lumber and stone for building, food to harvest, clay to mold. The muscles are alive to joy only in action, in climbing, running, skiing, and the like. Life finds its zest in overcoming, dominating, conquering some obstacle. It is the active deed that is satisfying, the deed that meets the challenge of the present, the daring and the adventuresome deed. Not in cautious foresight, not in relaxed ease does life attain completion. Outward energetic action, the excitement of power in the tangible present—this is the way to live.

Way 13: One should let oneself be used—used by other persons in their growth, used by the great objective purposes in the universe that silently and irresistibly achieve their goal. For persons' and the world's purposes are basically dependable and can be trusted. One should be humble, content, faithful, uninsistent; grateful for affection and protection but undemanding; close to persons and to nature, and willing to be second; nourishing the good by devotion. One should be a serene, confident, quiet vessel and instrument of the great dependable powers that move to fulfill themselves.

▸ VARIATION

After you have ranked each of these ways to live based on your personal preference, ask yourself the question "Which of these ways to live would make this a better world to live in for all the people of the world?" and rank all thirteen choices again based on that criterion. Then compare your new rankings with the first set of rankings you did and reflect upon any differences you may notice.

To use in a family or group, have each person share his or her rankings and responses with other family or group members.

68

Holiday Gift Giving

▶ **PURPOSE**

The Christmas or holiday season gives us a good opportunity to look at our patterns of gift giving. This strategy has us consider a unique alternative to our regular gift-giving pattern. However, this activity could really be done at any time during the year.

▶ **PROCEDURE**

On a sheet of paper, divide the paper into five columns. In the first column, list ten people who are very close to you. They can be family, friends, coworkers, and so on, but they ought to be ten people who touch your life frequently and with intensity.

In the second column, write the gift you gave that person last Christmas or holiday or the gift you plan on giving this year. If you didn't give them a Christmas or holiday gift, recall a gift you gave that person at another time during the year. If you haven't given that person any tangible gift in the last couple of years, just leave the space blank.

In the third column, list a gift you could give to each person that would dramatically change some aspect of that person's behavior. Perhaps it would be the gift of "Being able to listen better" or "Learning to laugh at the funny tricks life plays on you." Give each of these people a gift you think would make them happier, as well as changing their behavior.

In the fourth column, try to list some tangible gift you could give each person that would help them achieve the behavior change you listed in the third column. It could be a tangible gift, a poem, a letter you would write to them, a framed quotation for their wall—anything that might help them grow or change in the way that would make them happier. Take some time to think about this.

Finally, in the last column, list a gift that each of these people could give *you* to change one or more of *your* behavior patterns. Try to imagine what behavioral change each of the people you listed would like to endow you with. More than one person can give you the same gift. If you think you would get the same gift from all ten, it tells you something important.

Follow up by making an action plan for actually bringing about some of the changes noted above. For example, consider writing two Self-Contracts (Strategy Number 59, page 254), one of which involves giving one of the growth-producing gifts to one of the ten people on your gift list and one of which involves giving a growth-producing gift to yourself.

Past Christmas and Holiday Inventory

► **PURPOSE**

Christmas or the holiday season, like birthdays, comes every year. This exercise looks at Christmas/holiday card giving and can help make your future Christmas/holidays more consistent with your values.

► **PROCEDURE**

In January, bring in the Christmas/holiday cards you received that holiday season. Sort them out into several categories as follows:

Pile One is the stack of cards from people to whom you also sent a card.

Pile Two is from the people who sent you a card and to whom you had not originally sent a card but did send one after receiving theirs.

Pile Three is from people who sent you cards but to whom you did not send cards.

Also make a list of people to whom you sent a card and

who did not send you one and a second list of people who sent you a card but you suspect did so only after receiving one from you.

When this has been done, examine and reflect upon your Christmas/holiday card giving pattern. Then do I Learned Statements (Strategy Number 15, page 126).

Finally, make a Self-Contract (Strategy Number 59, page 254) about what you want to do about Christmas/holiday cards next Christmas/holiday season.

This exercise can also be combined with an Alternatives Search (Strategy Number 23, page 150) on "Alternatives to the Store-Bought Christmas/Holiday Card."

RRAs: Resent-Request-Appreciate*

► PURPOSE

Many of the conflicts we have with people close to us are values conflicts. It often boils down to the fact that we just see life differently. What you like, I don't like. What I want, you don't seem to want as much. A lot of these values conflicts generate strong feelings of resentment. This exercise attempts to teach one technique for handling feelings of resentment that grow out of values conflicts. You will learn to make what we call RRAs.

► PROCEDURE

Fold a paper into four long vertical columns. In the first column, list the ten people with whom you come into closest contact, day after day. You would probably list your family, your boss, your spouse/girlfriend or boyfriend, your best friends, your teacher, and so on. You can list more than ten or fewer than ten if you want to.

---

*Based on a technique learned from Janet Lederman.

In the second column, for at least three of the people on your list, write a sentence or two that expresses a resentment you have about some behavior trait they have. Don't be frightened by the word *resentment*. It's a real word and one our feelings understand well enough.

Begin your statements with the phrase "I resent it when . . . ." For example: "I resent it, Jim, when you don't do your share of the work around the house," or " I resent it, Doris, when you apple-polish our boss."

After you have written your three "I resent" statements, think about this idea: Behind every resentment we feel for someone else, there is an implied request we really want to make. We rarely have resentment by itself. There is something we want changed and we want it changed fast usually.

In the third column, try to write down the request you really have for each of the "I resent" statements you made. Make it specific and realistic. For example, "I resent it, Jim, when you don't do your share of work around the house, and I request that you take out the garbage on Tuesday nights and that you shovel the driveway when it snows."

The fourth column is for the "A" part of RRA. It means "appreciate." Our resentments and requests would actually mean more to the people we offer them to if we tried to see things from their point of view and appreciated why they behave as they do. For example, "I resent it, Jim, when you don't do your share of work around the house, and I request that you take out the garbage on Tuesday nights and that you shovel the driveway when it snows; but I do appreciate the fact that you are involved with so many activities that you sometimes don't have time and sometimes are so caught up in your activities that you don't remember."

Or "I resent it, Doris, when you apple-polish our boss, and I request that you regain your integrity and treat her with your honest feelings; but I appreciate the amazing skill you have of blatantly buttering her up without arousing the least suspicion in her."

Now write "I request" and "I appreciate" statements for the three people for whom you originally made "I resent" statements.

NOTE: You will note that in our examples, there have been two kinds of appreciation statements. One kind conveys empathy and lets the resented person know that you appreciate his or her side of the story, too. The other type of appreciation conveys an admiration for some aspect of the resented behavior. For example, "I resent it when you tell off-color jokes at parties, and I request that you cut it out; but I appreciate that you are a good storyteller and the jokes *are* pretty funny."

Some people are fearful of what will happen when they begin to allow their resentments to come out. But the resentments are there, interfering with your relationships anyway. Only by allowing them—yes, even encouraging them—to surface can they be dealt with. Dealing with strong feelings is an important part of the values-clarifying process, and we need every possible communication skill we can develop to express these feelings at an honest level for close examination. People who learn to use RRAs (and it must be stressed that all three parts are essential) seem to grow tremendously in their capacity to relate to and grapple with real values issues.

If you feel the word *resent* is too strong for the situation or the word *request* does not quite capture your meaning, you may substitute other words that better describe your feelings. For example, "It *bothers* me, Bob, when you use that expression. I *wish* you'd find a different way to say what you want to. I appreciate that you probably weren't even aware that it bothered me." You may be tempted to substitute the word *demand* for *request*, but unless you have made previous RRAs to no avail and you are really ready to issue an ultimatum, a request for change is more likely to succeed than a demand.

The request need not call for a specific behavior change. It can go something like, "I request we take some time to talk over the situation and work something out."

Ready for Summer

▸ PURPOSE

Summers are often menacing to people. They provide a long stretch of time in which we potentially can accomplish an amazing amount of work, learning, or playing. Yet, frequently we become frustrated because we're not having as much fun as we think we should or are not getting as much work done as we think we should. Setting realistic goals and "shoulds" is part of values clarification. Another part of the process, important for most people, is establishing some balance between fun and productivity. This exercise brings into focus the issue of realistic planning and apportioning of free time.

▸ PROCEDURE

Do this activity when you are beginning to think about or plan for the summer. Divide a sheet of paper into five columns headed by Roman numerals I through V.

Under Roman numeral I, list all the places you'd like to go this summer that you think would be fun. List beaches, mountains, towns, cities you'd like to visit. Make note of the people you like whom you would like to visit. You might also mention concert halls, stadiums, theaters, and so on. List all the places you really want to go.

Then, under Roman numeral II, list all the less-than-fun things you feel you have to get done. Do you have a house to paint? Dead trees to cut up into firewood? Unfinished office work or an "incomplete" to work off by doing a term paper? This category is for all the things you have to get done and that are not primarily fun.

Under Roman numeral III, list all the books you want to read this summer. Maybe there won't be any; but if you have been thinking of some, list them by title or by author.

Under Roman numeral IV, list anything you want to learn to do or get better at doing. List the skills that you plan to set aside some time for developing and improving.

Finally, under Roman numeral V, put down anything you want to make or produce, or have to show for the summer. It may be money, a painting, an article of clothing, an object or possession, a suntan. If you don't have anything to list, leave this topic blank.

When you have completed your lists, choose up to ten items—not more than two from any category—that you *really* want to do this summer, things that are high on your list of priorities. Put a star next to each of these.

For each of these starred items, answer the following questions:

1. What will I need in order to do it (e.g., money, pencil and paper, and so on)?
2. Is there anyone who can help me do it?
3. What are the first steps I will have to take?

4. What deadlines or schedule can I realistically set and stick to?

NOTE: You might resist inventories like this one. Interestingly, we have found that often a person who resists such an exercise is the one who has been rigid and compulsive and is now trying to be more flexible and spontaneous. Thoreau is frequently a model for such people, but they tend to forget Thoreau's delight in inventorying.

Are You Someone Who?

► **PURPOSE**

This strategy causes you to consider more thoughtfully what you value, what you want out of life, and what type of person you want to become.

► **PROCEDURE**

For each of the questions that follow or apply to you, answer "Yes," "No," or "Maybe" for each item. This is done by circling either Y, N, or M, which appear before each question.

After you have answered all the questions, choose one question that you answered with an emphatic "yes" or "no" and write about why you answered that way.

Finally, make a list of twenty "I Am Someone Who . . ." sentences. You may use ten of the items from the given list and make up ten new items, expressing personal goals and hopes you have for the future or values or behaviors you follow in the present.

▶ **THE QUESTIONS**

ARE YOU SOMEONE WHO . . . .

Y N M **1.** is likely to have six or more children?

Y N M **2.** will probably buy a new piece of technology every year?

Y N M **3.** is likely to become a PTA president?

Y N M **4.** will insist upon having wall-to-wall carpeting?

Y N M **5.** will travel to Europe?

Y N M **6.** will never want to go to Europe?

Y N M **7.** will probably wear long hair all of your life?

Y N M **8.** is likely to practice natural childbirth?

Y N M **9.** is likely to marry someone of another religion?

Y N M **10.** is likely to grow a beard some summer? (male)

Y N M   is likely to not shave your legs some summer? (female)

Y N M **11.** is likely to remain a virgin before you marry?

Y N M **12.** will always read the sports page?

Y N M **13.** will always read the comics?

Y N M **14.** will be a consistent writer of letters to the editor?

Y N M **15.** will marry for money?

Y N M **16.** will run for public office?

Y N M **17.** would be/is a difficult person to be married to?

Y N M **18.** would/did not consider getting engaged without a ring?

Y   N   M   **19.** is likely to publish a short story someday?

Y   N   M   **20.** is likely to play the lead in an amateur
theater group?

Y   N   M   **21.** is likely to get fat?

Y   N   M   **22.** watches a lot of TV?

Y   N   M   **23.** will insist on going to a restaurant at
least twice a week?

Y   N   M   **24.** will allow your male children to wear an
earring if they want to?

Y   N   M   **25.** will not permit your hair to gray naturally?

Y   N   M   **26.** is apt to go out of your way to have a
black (white) as a neighbor?

Y   N   M   **27.** will home-school your children?

Y   N   M   **28.** is apt to retire earlier than most people
do?

Y   N   M   **29.** will go to heaven?

ARE YOU SOMEONE WHO . . .

Y   N   M   **30.** will read/look at *Penthouse* magazine
when you get the chance?

Y   N   M   **31.** will never go out without shined shoes?

Y   N   M   **32.** will probably/did make a bad first marriage?

Y   N   M   **33.** will change your religion?

Y   N   M   **34.** is sure to move away from your
hometown?

Y   N   M   **35.** will make a career in the military?

Y   N   M   **36.** will probably live to a ripe old age?

Y   N   M   **37.** will refuse to live in a housing development?

Y   N   M   **38.** is apt to get into trouble with the law?

Y   N   M   **39.** is likely to turn out to be a liberal who became conservative? or the reverse?

Y   N   M   **40.** will never hire a cleaning person?

Y   N   M   **41.** may develop a drinking problem?

Y   N   M   **42.** will be likely to win a Nobel Peace Prize?

Y   N   M   **43.** locks all doors and windows when you are alone in the house?

Y   N   M   **44.** can't resist a bakery?

Y   N   M   **45.** has a rock group picture in your home?

Y   N   M   **46.** buys Bach tapes or CDs?

Y   N   M   **47.** is apt to experiment with pot?

Y   N   M   **48.** orders a soft drink rather than a cocktail when out socially?

Y   N   M   **49.** always wears seat belts?

Y   N   M   **50.** may contract a socially transmitted disease?

ARE YOU SOMEONE WHO . . .

Y   N   M   **51.** would get therapy on your own initiative?

Y   N   M   **52.** has insomnia?

Y   N   M   **53.** is apt to do anonymous favors for people?

Y   N   M   **54.** cheats on exams or income tax returns?

Y   N   M   **55.** brown-noses bosses/teachers?

Y   N   M   **56.** would lend your last subway token?

Y   N   M   **57.** is a thoughtful lover?

Y   N   M   **58.** would lie to save someone else's reputation?

Y   N   M   **59.** wakes up often with nightmares?

Y   N   M   **60.** could be satisfied without a college degree?

Y   N   M   **61.** knows little about birth control?

Y	N	M	**62.** will make a nervous mother? father?
Y	N	M	**63.** will make a faithful husband? wife?
Y	N	M	**64.** drives too fast?
Y	N	M	**65.** can't have fun at a party unless slightly drunk?
Y	N	M	**66.** will/may have been married more than once?
Y	N	M	**67.** would be a good teacher of very young children?
Y	N	M	**68.** is very materialistic?
Y	N	M	**69.** is a talking liberal/conservative who hasn't done anything?
Y	N	M	**70.** will make a wonderful father? mother?
Y	N	M	**71.** will never have as much money as you want?
Y	N	M	**72.** will never want much money?
Y	N	M	**73.** will change your hair color several times in your life?

ARE YOU SOMEONE WHO . . .

Y	N	M	**74.** will never go to a beauty parlor?
Y	N	M	**75.** will insist on a small wedding?
Y	N	M	**76.** is indifferent to food?
Y	N	M	**77.** will put sport jackets and ties on your three-year-old son?
Y	N	M	**78.** turns the radio on the minute you get into the room or car?
Y	N	M	**79.** can't quit the late show in the middle?
Y	N	M	**80.** never buys pornography?

I Wonder Statements (Strategy Number 16, page 128) can follow this exercise.

Who's to Blame?

► PURPOSE

We often get insight into our own lives by taking sides in someone else's conflict. This little story has much the same purpose as Alligator River (Strategy Number 50, page 230) and The Fallout-Shelter Problem (Strategy Number 48, page 222). It gets you to see what you are affirming and protecting in your own value structure.

► PROCEDURE

Here is a story in which you will meet several characters. You will be asked to rank order them, with the person most distasteful to you in the number 1 spot and the person least distasteful to you in the number 4 spot. Here is the story:

"There is a high school student who is selling marijuana to junior high school kids because he desperately needs money to get the transmission fixed on his car. He needs the car to get to his job as a busboy at the country club. The car he bought, it turns out, had its transmission filled with sawdust, which kept it running just long enough to get beyond the ten-day guarantee given to him by the used-car salesman. When confronted, the used-car salesman said, 'Look, that's just the way we took the car in. We didn't check it. We didn't do anything to it, good or bad. Go see the person who sold it to me.'

"The woman who sold the car to the used-car dealer sold it in a hurry because she bought a new house in the suburbs and had to raise the money for the closing costs quickly or her family would have been without a roof over its head. The car she sold was really their second car, and she was going to get around to getting the transmission fixed after they moved and got settled in their new house. But when the closing costs came due, she filled the transmission with sawdust and sold the car to the dealer for the wholesale book price. The used-car dealer cleaned the car up a bit and sold it to the high school student at the retail book price, making some money on the deal.

"The new house buyer said she wouldn't have done what she did if she hadn't been desperate, and she blamed the banker for not telling her well in advance what the closing costs would be.

"The banker said, 'Now, if she hadn't been so cheap, she would have hired a lawyer who knows all about closing costs, but she wanted to save a few bucks and do it herself. We handle too many deals here to be able to keep up with each individual who comes in for a mortgage. Anyhow, she ought to have known that there are always closing costs. But what can you expect from those kind of people? As soon as blacks begin moving into their neighborhoods, they rush out here to the suburbs like the plague was after them and they don't stop to think about details like closing costs, mortgage fees, and so on. Well, business is business, and we're in the business of lending money, we're not lawyers for people who don't know about closing costs.' "

Now your job is to rank order these people. Put the one you blame the most in the number 1 spot and the one you consider least blameworthy in the number 4 spot.

As a follow-up activity, write in your Values Journal (Strategy Number 17, page 130). Discuss the values, beliefs, or feelings you were protecting as evidenced by your rankings. In effect, ask yourself, "What do my rankings say to me about my values?"

In a family or group setting, the leader asks members to compare their individual rankings and discuss differences and similarities.

Brand Names

► **PURPOSE**

One of the functions of values-clarification procedures is to bring to a conscious level the choices we make. Often we allow ourselves to fall into patterns of choosing without ever really examining them. This strategy asks you to look at your own pattern and at your family's pattern of buying to see how many of the valuing processes went into each choice.

► **PROCEDURE**

Prepare three worksheets as follows:

► **WORKSHEET ONE**

ALL THE BRAND NAMES IN OUR MEDICINE CABINET	I	II	III
1.			
2.			
3.			
4.			
5.			

ALL THE BRAND NAMES IN OUR MEDICINE CABINET	I	II	III
6.			
7.			
8.			
9.			
10.			
Etc.			

► **WORKSHEET TWO**

ALL THE BRAND NAMES IN OUR CANNED GOODS CABINET	I	II	III
1.			
2.			
3.			
4.			
5.			
6.			
7.			
8.			
9.			
10.			
Etc.			

▶ **WORKSHEET THREE**

ALL THE BRAND NAMES IN OUR GARAGE	I	II	III
1.			
2.			
3.			
4.			
5.			
6.			
7.			
8.			
9.			
10.			
ETC.			

Then list all the brand names you find in these three places. List every brand name, not just the well-known brand names. If you don't have a garage, think of your yard, driveway, and/or storage area.

In Column I, write the name of the person who most likely chose that particular brand. How did it get into the house? Who brought it in?

In Column II, explain why that particular brand was chosen. Start with the items that you yourself introduced into the house and try to identify who or what influenced you to buy that particular brand. Was it a recommendation from a friend? Did a salesman sell it to you? Did you buy it because you saw it advertised? Where? Write in Column

II, as best you can, who or what motivated you to buy that particular brand. Then ask other people in your family, the ones who bought or introduced each brand into your home, what made them choose that particular brand. Try to find some explanation for each item on your list and place it in Column II.

In Column III, place a check if the item was picked by making use of these three criteria: It was chosen after examining several alternatives. It was chosen after thoughtfully considering the pros and cons of the alternatives. It was a free choice, not a pressured one.

Finally, review your list to examine how vulnerable you are to the mass media and to the pitchman's magic.

NOTE: Don't get defensive or feel guilty if many of your purchases seem to indicate that you are gullible to the Madison Avenue hustler. The truth is, we are all vulnerable, but we can be less so if we begin to use the values criteria when we buy.

Younger children can learn a lot by doing a brand-name survey of all their toys. They will learn that television has done an incredible job of getting them to want the latest Barbie doll costume, the newest Hot Wheels car, and so on.

Teenagers and adults can also examine the brand names of books or recordings they have bought and the labels of clothes in their closets.

A fourth column can be added. In this column, write one of the following code letters:

K = I'll *keep* it or keep buying it.
E = I'll *eliminate* it or stop buying it.

C = I'll *change* to another brand.
T = I'll have to *think* more about whether I'll keep it, eliminate it, or change to another brand.

A good follow-up for this strategy is Baker's Dozen (Strategy Number 75, page 307).

Baker's Dozen

► **PURPOSE**

A theme that runs all through these strategies is that in order to make some sense out of the bewildering array of alternatives in our life, we have to set some priorities. This strategy gets at this issue in a fresh way.

► **PROCEDURE**

On a sheet of paper, make a list of thirteen things (a baker's dozen) that you personally use around your house that make use of electricity. This includes anything at all with plugs that you, yourself, use fairly frequently.

Now draw a line through the three things you could live without the easiest. If, for example, there was an acute power shortage and every home was asked to cut down on its use of electricity, which three could you give up most easily? These are the three you'd cross out.

On the other hand, which three do you find the most precious? Draw a circle around these items. These would be the last ones you would want to give up. Then make l

Learned Statements (Strategy Number 15, page 126) about these thirteen possessions or about your material possessions in general.

▶ **VARIATIONS**

Instead of, or in addition to, electrical appliances, you could list thirteen phonograph records, CDs, or tapes you own, identifying the three most important and the three least important items. Or you could list thirteen items of clothing in your closet or thirteen articles of furniture or decor in your home. In each case, choose the three you could most easily give up and the three you regard as most valuable.

You might also consider whether you would give any of the three items you crossed out to needy individuals or families.

STRATEGY 76

Reaction Statements

▸ PURPOSE

This strategy causes you to thoughtfully consider a variety of values issues and, if in a family or group setting, to publicly affirm your reactions to these issues.

▸ PROCEDURE

When you see or hear a thought-provoking statement, write it down and then later, or at the time, write your reaction to the statement. Or select one of the Reaction Statements we have provided below and write your reaction to it.

In a family or group setting, choose one of these statements and read your reaction to it to the other family or group members.

▸ SAMPLE REACTION STATEMENTS

1. Adults get paid for their work. Kids should get paid for going to school. How about fifty cents an hour?
2. Thou shalt not kill, except in wars.

3. "Most men lead lives of quiet desperation."—Thoreau
4. If a parent catches his child smoking marijuana, he/she should turn the child over to the civil authorities so he/she can be helped.
5. There were over 50,000 deaths in auto accidents last year on U.S. highways.
6. Women are really the stronger sex.
7. Students should be allowed to use curse words in the school newspaper if this will help them make a serious point.
8. Premarital sexual intercourse is wrong.
9. The world is going to hell in a handbasket.
10. "Three strikes and you're out." (That is, felons convicted of three violent crimes should be sent to prison for life.)

► ADDITIONAL REACTION STATEMENTS

The thirty-five Strongly Agree/Strongly Disagree statements in Strategy 40 (page 200) all make excellent Reaction Statements.

Index of Strategies

About the Authors

The authors have been helping individuals, groups, and organizations clarify their values since the 1960s. SIDNEY SIMON (Old Mountain Road, Hadley, MA 01035) is a professor emeritus at University of Massachusetts. LELAND HOWE (Box 745, E. Lansing, MI 48826) is a bioenergetic therapist in private practice. HOWARD KIRSCHENBAUM (458 Whiting Road, Webster, NY 14580) is an adjunct faculty member in the Department of Education and Human Development, State University of New York at Brockport. All are active consultants to schools, nonprofit organizations, and businesses in the field of values, organizational development, and other topics.

Collectively, Drs. Simon, Howe, and Kirschenbaum have written or coauthored forty books in the fields of education, psychology, and history, including: Simon, Howe, and Kirschenbaum's *Values Clarification: A Handbook of Practical Strategies for Teachers and Students* (New York: Hart, 1972, 1978); Simon's *Getting Unstuck* (New York: Warner Books, 1992); Howe's *Raising Children in a TV World* (New York: Hart, 1978), and Kirschenbaum's *100 Ways to Enhance Values and Morality in Schools and Youth Settings* (Needham Heights, MA: Allyn and Bacon, 1995).

The authors may be reached at the addresses above for further information about their work or other publications.

If you are interested in attending a workshop on Values Clarification or other topics, please write for a current schedule to: Values Realization Institute, Box 230, Hadley, MA 01035.